LAWYERS ON THEIR OWN

LAWYERS
on Their Own

*A study of individual practitioners
in Chicago*

JEROME E. CARLIN

Rutgers University Press, New Brunswick
NEW JERSEY

This book was manufactured with the assistance
of a grant from The Ford Foundation.

Acknowledgment is made to West Publishing Company
for permission to quote from
The American Law School Review.

To my parents

Preface

This is a book about a particular kind of lawyer, his work, his problems, and his aspirations.

Although conceived initially as a study in the sociology of the professions, as time went on the study began to shape itself more as a report to the public and to the legal profession itself on what actually is going on in the practice of law. It seemed to me both groups were badly in need of a realistic picture of law practice—the public in order to appraise more intelligently the functions of the profession upon which it must depend for the preservation of its rights and liberties, the bar to enable it to take whatever actions are necessary to put its house in order.

The report that follows is based primarily on information obtained from close to one hundred interviews I personally conducted in the summer of 1957 with a sample of

Chicago lawyers practicing on their own. I decided to limit the study to individual practitioners partly out of convenience (being limited in time and resources I thought it best to avoid the complications of practice and organization in firms), partly because the majority of lawyers in Chicago as in most other cities in the United States are still individual practitioners, and finally, because I was curious to see how these bearers of the traditional image of the free, independent professional were faring in the contemporary metropolitan bar.

The sample was drawn at random from a directory of lawyers (see Appendix A for discussion of sampling procedures). I took a random sample not so much for statistical reasons as to insure the representative character of the interviews. The interviews generally took place in the office of the respondent and lasted on the average about two hours. I was guided in the interview by a schedule consisting mostly of open-ended questions (see Appendix B). The answers were taken down verbatim. By and large the lawyers were extremely cooperative and far more candid than I had expected, their own colleagues' admonitions to the contrary notwithstanding. Many seemed to be genuinely interested in the study, although highly skeptical that any meaningful regularities could be found in their work. Finally, I had the definite impression that these lawyers were extremely delighted that someone had taken the trouble to get their story, a story that they were very eager to tell.

Needless to say, some caution should be exercised in generalizing from findings based on such a small sample of lawyers taken from one segment of the bar in a single city. Two things, however, should be emphasized in this regard: First, that in making a qualitative study in depth I was less concerned about the number of interviews than about what I could learn from any single interview. Second, in my current study of the New York City bar, which is based upon a sample of 800 lawyers, there is nothing to suggest that what I found to be true about individual lawyers in Chicago is unique to Chicago.

Of the many people who helped to make this study possible I am especially grateful to the lawyers in my sample who gave so generously of their most valuable commodity —their time. Without their cooperation, their willingness to explore with me the intricacies of their practice, and perhaps most important, their candor in discussing the problems of their work, this book very obviously could not have been written.

Particular thanks are due also to Everett C. Hughes, now at Brandeis University, and to Harry Kalven, Jr. and Peter Rossi, of the University of Chicago, for guidance and assistance during the various stages of the study; to Allen H. Barton, Director of the Bureau of Applied Social Research, Columbia University, whose many invaluable suggestions and criticisms I could not possibly enumerate; to Edward Shils of the University of Chicago and Howard S. Becker of Stanford University for their most opportune encouragement; to Bernard Berelson of the Population Council, and Alex Elson, member of the Illinois Bar, for their reading of and comments on an earlier draft of the manuscript; and to Dan C. Lortig of Harvard University, Frederick B. Mc-Kinnon of the American Bar Foundation, Saul H. Mendlovitz of Rutgers Law School, Erwin O. Smigel of New York University, and Wagner P. Thielins, Jr. of the Bureau of Applied Social Research—all fellow researchers in the legal profession who in the course of many pleasant exchanges have helped me immeasurably in formulating and refining my ideas about the legal profession.

I would like to express my appreciation also to John C. Leary, Director of the American Bar Foundation, for his kind permission to use the facilities of the Foundation in the preparation of the manuscript.

JEROME E. CARLIN

New York, New York
August, 1962

Contents

LAWYERS ON THEIR OWN

1

The Road to Individual Practice

The individual practitioner of law in Chicago is a self-made man who came up the hard way from poor, immigrant surroundings. His father, generally an immigrant from Eastern Europe with little or no formal education, was in most cases the proprietor of a small business.[1] The one burning ambition of the son was to escape from the ghetto, to rise above his father, to become a professional man. Again and again, in answer to the question of what led them to become lawyers, respondents revealed this strong drive for professional status:

> I never had any visions of glamor or glory, but a profession, honorable, making a living. My uncle [a lawyer] was living comfortably and had standing in the community. I came from poor circumstances, my father was ill many years, and my brother and I had to support the family. We became professional men [his brother is also

a lawyer] . . . a tremendous thing, especially during the depression. (11) *

I was in a big family of 13 children. When I was 12 I quit school—after two years of high school—to go to work. I was going to make a living for the family. I was doing fairly well, a shipping clerk, $15 a week. I was promised a dollar a week more if I would stay and not go back to school. But I decided to go back to school, in 1923. I decided to have a specific profession, I had no idea of any other profession. (94)

I wanted to be a lawyer, and the family wanted me to be one—although since then I've realized that monetarily you can do a lot better in business. Jewish people think it's very important to be a professional, and I was always a big talker. (35)

Principally it was a question of going into some pursuit that involved respect, dignity. Among Jewish people professions are very important. And with my parents, they had little or no education, their children should have professions. There was a certain amount of appeal. Professional men were looked up to then. At one time in former years, the almighty dollar was not as important as it is today. (64)

Well over half the lawyers interviewed claimed they had no specific intention of becoming lawyers. Most of them confessed that they came to the law by default, having abandoned the idea of going into medicine, engineering, or one of a variety of other professional pursuits because they found them to be too expensive, academically too demanding, or because they saw themselves barred by discrimination.

* A number in parentheses is the author's identification of the respondent.

I had been taking all sorts of courses at Crane [Junior College], I didn't know what I was going to be. When I put 'em together I had sufficient for pre-law. That's how I studied law instead of medicine. I wanted to be a doctor but I was too lazy—not that I wasn't a good student, I just didn't get around to it. I'm a pretty fair student. (30)

I decided the day I entered law school. I was thinking of medicine, dentistry, or even pharmacy. Through high school and college I had a narrow education, I couldn't go anywhere on it, except into sales. I didn't get into medical school or dental school. Law was my third choice. (25)

Interviewer: When did you decide to become a lawyer?
Respondent: I suppose in 1933, when I entered law school. I considered engineering, but funds were not available for engineering.
Interviewer: Did you want to be a lawyer?
Respondent: Not particularly. I preferred engineering.
Interviewer: Did you have any idea of the kind of work lawyers did or the kind of work you might be doing?
Respondent: Not at all, not the remotest idea. (82)

A Negro lawyer said engineering had been his first choice also:

I wanted to be an engineer, but I would have had to go to Argentina to cash in on it, so I went into law as a second choice. (75)

A similar experience was reported by a Jewish lawyer:

I wanted to be a chemical engineer but my college professors said it was no place for a Jew.
Interviewer: Why did you decide on the law?
Respondent: Family, I guess.

Interviewer: Are there any lawyers in your family?
Respondent: My brother was a lawyer.
Interviewer: Did you want to be a lawyer, or was it something you fell into?
Respondent: A combination, both; I gravitated. (14)

The individual practitioner in Chicago has in most cases received his professional training in one of the "proprietary" or Catholic night law schools.[2] Although most of those who went on to a night law school had only a year or two of college credit (if that) from either a downtown night extension school or a local junior college,[3] they encountered little difficulty in gaining admission into the notoriously low-standard night law schools and faced relatively few obstacles in getting through them.

Requirements for admission to the night law school during the twenties and thirties (when two out of three of the respondents entered law school) were practically nonexistent. The general rule in such institutions was to accept any person with a high school diploma or "its equivalent," which frequently meant accepting someone with fewer than four years of high school.[4] The concern of many such schools of that period was not in keeping out the unqualified student but in recruiting as many students as possible regardless of qualifications.

Scholastic standards suffered not only from the absence of any definite rule on exclusions but also from an unwillingness to fail a poor student. Courses of instruction were limited to subjects covered by the state bar examinations, and the instructors, most of whom conducted a full-time law practice during the day, rarely had the time or the inclination to prepare for their classes.

No better summary of the character and quality of the night law school at this time can be found than in an address given in 1933 at the thirty-first annual meeting of the Association of American Law Schools in Chicago by Will Shafroth, an indefatigable crusader in the field of legal education:

> Here indeed [in the area of legal training] we find a wilderness, and if we look around it, what do we see? A veritable host of degree-conferring law schools, less than 40 per cent of them wearing the ribbon of merit which membership in the Association of American Law Schools confers, and only eight more, or a total of 84 . . . out of 194, being on the American Bar Association's roll of honor. Last year [1932] the attendance in these approved schools was 46 per cent of the total law school attendance. In other words, we are obliged to admit that more than half of our law students [93 per cent of whom were in night law schools [5]] are getting the kind of training which the leaders in the teaching profession . . . regard as inadequate.
>
> Isn't that statement in itself astounding? We rail about the character of the bar, at the difficulties in securing law reform, at ambulance chasing and lack of ethics, at professional incompetence, and yet we expect improvement while we are fostering, in the great majority of the states of the Union, schools which exploit their students for their own financial gain, and send them to the bar inadequately prepared, giving to the bar examiners the impossible task of turning back time after time those who are not qualified.
>
> It may be that our judgment of what is and what is not proper preparation for the bar is at fault. Arbitrary standards are never perfect in their discriminative functions. But what can we say of those schools which ignore all the rules of experience, which admit students who have had only a high school education or what they claim for an equivalent, and which have a course of three years or less

of evening sessions, or less than three years of full-time work. There are 38 of these schools which confer degrees scattered over the country, and some 15 others which do not. [Most were night law schools.[6]] Every one of them is a commercial school, designed first to make a profit, and, only secondarily, and in such ways as will not interfere with that profit, to teach law. I have never seen a school in that category, that is, failing in both entrance requirements and length of course as viewed from our standards, which I regarded as a fit place for a man to study law. . . . The fact that these law schools continue to exist and turn out their yearly grist is nothing short of a tragedy.[7]

Ironically, in spite of the poor showing of the night law school graduates in the bar examination almost all were eventually admitted to practice. Thus, for example, of all the candidates who took the bar examination in the years 1922 through 1924 in New York, Pennsylvania, Illinois, and California, 83 to 95 per cent had passed the bar examination by 1932, although less than half had passed on the first try. "The persistent candidate," it has been noted, "by cramming for the examination, by taking quiz courses and by coming back again and again will eventually succeed." [8]

In general, the individual practitioner works for another lawyer as a kind of apprentice during his first few years out of law school.[9] These are usually temporary positions—rarely lasting more than a year or two—paying little or, in the case of the space-for-service arrangement, no salary, the assumption being that the young lawyer will be building up his own practice on the side.[10] The employers—in nearly all cases either individual or small firm lawyers—appear to be primarily interested in getting an inexpensive legman, someone to run their errands in the clerks' offices, to make perfunctory court appearances, to help prepare their routine papers and documents, and occasionally to do some research. The young lawyer, on the other hand, becomes acquainted with the courts and local agencies; he gets to know his way around—whom to see and how to approach them. In other words, he gets an initiation into the workings of the lower-level judicial and administrative bureaucracies.

> As a law clerk I got no particular attention from them [his employers], but I learned from them.
> *Interviewer:* You mean your way around the courts?
> *Respondent:* Yes, but law too, pleadings and depositions. The big important thing, when you go around and see—at Christmastime it's traditional in Chicago to pass out $25 in envelopes to the clerks of court, the clerks in other offices, the bailiffs. If you don't, you're out of it. (25)

> I worked with ———— and ————, older men. I followed them around. I did legwork; I was the clerk in the firm. I got experience, contact with the courts. I was helped by coming here. You can't do it by yourself. You must associate yourself with men who have experience. Fifty per cent of your value in Chicago depends on who you know across the street [City Hall and County Buildings]. If you absorb it from someone who knows it, that's 50 per cent of the battle. If you associate yourself you just find out sooner: who to go to, where and how to go. For example, one thing you don't learn [in law school] is what papers you file in lawsuits. You need forms to file, and you have to know where to file them. The same with following return days, books of entry in City Hall, trial dates—the actual, the practical. Here's a summons you get [indicating a form]—what do you do with it? Well, you have to file an appearance. You go across the street and get a form.

You have to file in a certain window. Later you have to look and find who is assigned to it, and on what date. It's not difficult but you have to learn it and remember it, and that you get from actual doing. (30)

The relationship between the older lawyer and his "apprentice" is frequently less than harmonious. Many of those who worked for other lawyers reported unpleasant experiences: either that contact with their employer had led to disenchantment or, in most instances, that there had been open conflict with their employer. One lawyer who came out of law school in the midst of the Depression recalled:

I was in a space-for-service arrangement in an office with four attorneys. I had a sad experience—one that influenced me adversely. These three, or four, attorneys were former politicians. They had all held jobs under Republican regimes and they were sitting and waiting for the Republicans to get back in power in Chicago. One had been with the Sanitary District (and there had been a scandal). The other one ran unsuccessfully for Municipal Court judge. They were waiting to get back to the lush days. It was a disappointment to me, being a youngster out of law school with strong ambitions about law practice and some mistaken notions about it. This was my first contact with active lawyers on a business basis. These fellows were frustrated individuals, lawyers for many years but it still was a struggle—worrying about the rent and so on. That would be discouraging to all but the very strong-ambitioned individuals. Here these men with nothing, still struggling—but that was in '36 and '38 when the law practice was at a low ebb.

Interviewer: What were your mistaken ideas about law practice?

> *Respondent:* I thought that most lawyers were successful. (59)

Several reported conflicts over salary or over financial arrangements in general. One said that he felt he hadn't been paid enough for his services and that he had little chance for advancement within the small firm that employed him. After four years he finally decided to quit:

> My bosses were cheap bastards. . . . I had no chance to grow; I would never be more than I was. And they weren't giving anything away. When there was a big fee—I worked on one that brought in a $20,000 fee—they never gave us an extra bonus. (60)

Another, who worked for an active promoter in the local tax field—handling most of the paper work while his boss did the promoting—when asked why he left, stated:

> I was very dissatisfied. I collected in fees the second year I was there over $600,000 and I got $25 a week. It was unfair. I quit without having another job. When I told him I was going to leave he said, "Aren't you happy here?" I said: "No." "Why," he said, "is it the money?" "Almost nothing else," I said. "How much are you making?" he asked. I told him $25 a week and that I couldn't manage on that. Well, he went up to $50, $75, even $100 but I said *no.* (6)

Another had been clerk for a firm of eight lawyers for five years when he decided to quit:

> *Interviewer:* Why did you leave the firm?
> *Respondent:* There was a financial argument. I wanted

more money—at least that was part of it. The head of the firm had a theory you could always hire talent, and if you didn't bring in business there was a limit to what he would pay. I couldn't bring in business, and what I did bring in, there was a question of who got the fees. (14)

Another lawyer who had been dissatisfied with his work (he found that he was handling only eviction cases) and with his employers ("one boss knew less than I did; today he's a millionaire"), when asked why he finally left, replied:

There was a disagreement. One of the bosses thought I was holding back [the respondent was supposed to turn over 35 per cent of the fees he brought in from his own practice], which I wasn't, and I told him to go to hell. (19)

While these clerkships do not always end in conflict and mutual recrimination, there seem to be very strong pressures leading in that direction. In large measure these pressures arise from the part-time, temporary character of the position. In most instances the young lawyer will have some practice of his own which he is attempting to expand, and he usually finds it difficult to draw the line between his own time and the time he should give to his employer —and unless he devotes himself wholly to his employer, the situation can only grow less certain, requiring frequent redefinition of the terms of employment. The employer is often more than happy to permit his clerk to develop his own practice (up to a point), since this justifies a low salary. This arrangement, however, soon places the clerk in a potentially competitive relationship with his employer, particularly in view of the fact that whatever gap there may be between older and younger lawyer in terms of competence and business-getting ability is, at this level of the bar, relatively quickly bridged.

For most individual practitioners, getting started on their own was a hard, uphill struggle. Their work in the early years consisted generally of the dregs of legal practice and their income was correspondingly meager. The matters they handled were with few exceptions the least desirable from every point of view: the marginal cases, the cases no one else wanted, the cases involving the least return and the most aggravation.

> *Interviewer:* What were the problems of getting started on your own?
> *Respondent:* Getting clients that were paying clients. There are enough that float around from lawyer to lawyer who just want to check up on another lawyer—the junk. (35)

> The main problem was development of a clientele, and then obtaining lucrative business. A young lawyer is always recommended for small collections, dead judgments, and so on. (94)

> There's a lot of business around that it don't pay to handle. After a while you get independent. A lot of people want you to handle their business at your expense. (64)

Collection matters, evictions, rent cases, "dead" judgments, along with some personal injury, criminal, and divorce cases are the kinds of work most frequently handled in the early years in practice. The most distinguishing feature of such cases is their petty character—the small amount of money involved, the tenuousness of the claim (or its nonexistence)—and the inordinate amount of time required to make any headway at all. In short, such practice constitutes the dirty work, the "crap," the "junk" that no one else will handle, but which the younger lawyer will often have to take if he wants any business at all.

The indications are that income in the early years barely reaches a subsistence level. One lawyer reported an average of $2,500 his first two years out of law school; several said that they averaged less than $3,000 over the first four or five years, and many earned less than $100 a month the first six or eight months in practice. In many instances, of course, these lawyers had additional sources of income, but the notion of starving through the first few years is probably not far from the truth.

The kinds of work most young lawyers get when they first start out, the sources of their business, and the problems they have in making ends meet is well illustrated by the case of a young respondent just going into his second year of practice. Let us call him Ronald.

Ronald was admitted to practice in 1956 and over a period of the next eighteen months he had three jobs working for other lawyers. Before coming to his present position he had an informal arrangement with some friends that he hoped would lead to a partnership, but one of them backed down because he didn't want to share some of his "lucrative matters."

At present Ronald is in a space-for-service arrangement in a downtown office with two other lawyers, one of whom is rarely in the office. About a fifth of his time is devoted to doing legwork for the active lawyer in the office and another six or seven hours a week are given to a lawyer outside the office who pays him on an hourly basis. The rest of his time is his own to build up his own practice.

Interviewer: What is the nature of your practice?

Respondent: [Looking through his clients' file folders piled on top of his desk and in the drawers] I do all the subrogation work for an insurance company. I have 300 files in the drawer. There's supposed to be $3,000 worth of claims there; a third is mine, but most are uncollectable. It's a lot of work for the income involved.

Interviewer: How did you get these cases?

Respondent: My brother-in-law's brother knows an attorney who has a half interest in the insurance company. [Continuing through his files:]

Hardware store—collections.

A real estate deal for my milkman.

A will and trust matter for my sister-in-law's neighbor's mother.

My sister-in-law's aunt—personal injury.

This is for my sister-in-law's mother. I will do some estate planning—draw up a will and have some shares of stock transferred.

A case for ——— [lawyer for whom he works in the office]. The owner of a trailer claims a faulty installation, a suit for damages.

——— [other lawyer in the office] was in an auto accident.

My brother-in-law was in an auto accident.

I bought a washer and dryer at an appliance store. I asked them if they had any work for me. They gave me a few matters. I hope to get them for a retainer client. If only I had a few small retainers then I'd be okay. Otherwise, it's very sporadic.

Personal injury for my wife's aunt—auto accident.

Personal injury for a friend.

Personal injury for a friend—adulterated food.

Here's my star client—I've thrown her out a hundred times. I'm handling a bunch of things for her. She's not satisfied with a tuck-pointing job in one of her buildings; I called him up and got him to agree to a compromise. Personal property tax for a shoe store she owns. Default judgment against a shoe store; I'll have that vacated. Her son and daughter-in-law got sick from a bad pizza. A precinct captain broke a window in her building; I know him and he'll fix it. I haven't got any fees from her yet. They'll start coming in soon, though.

An immigration matter—I referred it to another attorney and I'm splitting a fee on it.

That's the extent of my practice now.

In his first year out of law school Ronald earned $3,000 from the practice of law. In addition, he made a little over $1,000 as a telephone solicitor for a storm window concern. The first month of the second year he made $50, and in the second, $400. He has a wife and two children, and is having difficulty paying his bills.

It's really touch and go. I don't know whether I'll make it. I may have to give up the practice. . . . I could make a lot more doing something else. I was offered $10,000 at the lumber yard, and I had a $7,500 offer from the Illinois Commerce Commission.

Interviewer: Why haven't you taken either of them?

Respondent: I don't know. I ask myself that. That's what we talk about—my friends and I—three of my cronies and I—we have coffee every morning and talk about our practice and our problems. If you're a salesman, it doesn't sound so good. It's a matter of pride or ego. I like the law, but it's not a burning thing in my life—I *must* be a lawyer. If I quit now I'd be admitting defeat. I'd be ashamed. . . . It's a nice profession, nice clean work, a respected profession. If I could get some income it would be a good life. You can get away when you want to play golf, and you're your own boss, that appeals to me. And if people ask you what you're doing it's nice to tell them I'm a lawyer, and not a clerk in a store. And my dad gets satisfaction from the fact that I'm a lawyer. (2)

One cannot fully understand the nature of individual practice without first recognizing where and how the individual practitioner fits into the wider structure of the metropolitan bar.

Although half the lawyers in Chicago, as in practically all the other cities of the United States, are individual practitioners,[11] they constitute something like a lower class of the metropolitan bar. The elite of the metropolitan bar is composed of lawyers in the larger firms. These firms have a virtual monopoly of the largest, most lucrative clients—the large corporations whose legal needs they are geared to serve—and of the best qualified lawyers. In hiring lawyers they aspire to the ideal of the giant Wall Street firms of selecting only the top graduates of Harvard, Yale, and Columbia law schools and of bringing them into the firm as soon after they graduate as possible.[12] In Chicago, New York, Boston, Philadelphia, Cleveland, San Francisco, and Los Angeles, for example, at least one out of four lawyers in firms with over 25 lawyers is a Harvard, Yale, or Columbia Law School graduate (principally Harvard), and almost all the others are graduates of the top local university law schools.[13]

The practice of most metropolitan individual practitioners is consequently confined to those residual matters (and clients) that the large firms have not pre-empted: (1) matters not large enough or remunerative enough for the large firms to handle—most general work for small to medium-sized businesses and corporations, the smaller real estate transactions (for individuals or small businesses), and estate matters for middle-income families; (2) the undesirable cases, the dirty work, those areas of practice that have associated with them an aura of influencing and fixing and that involve arrangements with clients and others that are felt by the large firms to be professionally damaging. The latter category includes local tax, municipal, personal injury, divorce, and criminal matters.

Individual practitioners come off second best not only with respect to type of practice but also in terms of quality of training and academic achievement. In Chicago, as we have seen, the majority of individual practitioners have had less than two years of undergraduate training, and two out of three are graduates of night law schools. This pattern seems to prevail in other large cities as well. In New York, Boston, Philadelphia, Cleveland, San Francisco, and Los Angeles 40 to 70 per cent of the individual practitioners are night law school graduates—compared with less than 15 per cent of the lawyers in firms of over 25 lawyers in these same cities.[14]

The rigidity of the class structure of the metropolitan bar is evidenced by the fact that those who start out as individual practitioners rarely become associates or partners in the larger firms. Moreover, most lawyers who are at present individual practitioners entered the profession as such (or as employees of such lawyers) and have remained at that level of practice.[15]

Between the big firm elite and the mass of individual practitioners is a stratum composed of lawyers in small to medium-sized firms. While it is difficult to distinguish the majority of these lawyers from individual practitioners in terms of social background, training, and type of practice, it is likely that the middle-sized firms, at any rate, may constitute something like a middle class of the metropolitan bar.[16]

The sharp classlike divisions in the metropolitan bar have come about as the result of historical developments beginning around the turn of the century. A factor of major importance has been the emergence of the large law firm as the principal form of organization for the leading purveyors of legal services to the business elite. Until the end of the nineteenth century there were probably no firms with more than half a dozen lawyers.[17] The period from the turn of the century to World War I witnessed the first substantial growth of law firms, with some firms in the larger East Coast cities expanding to as many as 20 or 30 lawyers. But the large firm as we know it today did not appear until the twenties, when metropolitan lawyers in increasing numbers were being called upon to shape the legal framework of the emerging economy of the giant corporation. The increased magnitude and complexity of the legal and general business advice required for the operation of these new giants necessitated a degree of specialization and concentration of legal talent that could be realized only in a very large firm. During the twenties, in New York, Chicago, and the other major cities of the country, law firms previously of 10 or 20 lawyers grew in size to 40, 50, and in some cases to as many as 70 lawyers.[18] The 1929 crash may have momentarily toppled the corporate structures that the large firms had so ingeniously assisted in creating, but the Depression and the flood of governmental controls and regulations that it brought about cemented further the interdependence between the large firm and big business and lent additional assurance to the permanence and importance of the big firm.

The establishment of the elite segment of the metropolitan bar in the newly emerging large firms ensured its monopoly of the largest and most influential business and commercial clients, largely because the smaller firms with their limited resources found it more and more difficult to compete for this kind of business. Furthermore, with the initiation of hiring policies that virtually required certain kinds of legal education for admission to the large firm, entry into the ranks of the elite became increasingly restricted. Thus, from their inception at the turn of the century, the largest firms have placed considerable weight on law school background and performance in selecting associates and partners.[19] Since 1895, for example, practically all the partners in the New York firm of Cravath, Swaine and Moore have been graduates of either Harvard, Yale, or Columbia Law School and roughly two out of three of their associates over the years have been from the same schools.[20] In the Sullivan and Cromwell firm only one partner from the date of its inception to 1920 was not a graduate of either Harvard or Columbia Law School. In a foreword to the history of the firm John Foster Dulles, whose law degree was from George Washington University, recalled the difficulties he encountered in trying to get into a prominent firm.

> I went to New York armed with letters of introduction from my grandfather, John W. Foster, to the heads of certain New York law firms whom he had come to know through his own wide experience in diplomacy and international affairs. These letters served to give me a courteous reception, but not a job. A degree from Princeton was an acceptable credential so far as concerned undergraduate work. But collegiate honors counted for little. The Sorbonne counted for nothing and George Washington Law School was unknown to New York. Law degrees from

Harvard or Columbia were, at that time, the requirement
for admission to the eminent law firms of New York.[21]

The increasing emphasis that the large firms were plac-
ing on type and quality of professional training in the
selection of partners and associates was undoubtedly facilitated by the change-over, around the turn of the century,
from law office apprenticeship to formal law school training for the bar.[22] It was obviously much simpler to dis-
criminate among recruits in terms of the law school they
had attended than the type of law office in which they had
apprenticed. In addition, the law schools provided a convenient measure of competence in their ratings of students
by academic achievement.

Mobility into the elite stratum of the metropolitan bar
was further limited during this period by a shift in the
central focus of law practice from the courtroom to the
conference and negotiation room, a development that
accompanied the growth of large-scale corporate enterprise
and the expansion of government control and regulation
of business. As a result of this shift, the ambitious young
lawyer of humble origin lost what had once been the most
accessible and effective forum for demonstrating his ability
to prospective clients of prestige and wealth. Thereafter
courtroom demonstrations of ability for the most part led
to prominence only in the less respected areas of practice
that had been either discarded or passed over by the larger
firms. Prominence in the respectable areas of practice and
access to important clients were more and more to be
gained only through association with the large firm.

During this period of the consolidation of the big firm
elite, changes of the greatest importance were also taking
place at the lower level of the metropolitan bar. The first

was the change-over from law office apprenticeship to night law school training for members of this part of the bar.[23] The second was a spectacular increase in the number of such lawyers. During the twenties, the period of maximum growth in this century of the profession as a whole,[24] the size of the bar in the ten largest cities increased by well over 50 per cent.[25] This marked expansion was effected largely by the influx into the ranks of the individual practitioners of the graduates from the rapidly expanding night law schools.[26]

A third development was the shift in the ethnic composition of this part of the bar from lawyers of predominantly German and Irish to Eastern European—largely Jewish—origin.[27] This continuation of the process of ethnic succession, with newer immigrant groups moving into the lower stratum of the bar, was apparently facilitated by the change-over to night law school training for the bar. It was doubtless easier for the sons of these more recent immigrants to gain admission to a night law school, the only requirement for which was the tuition fee, than to find a preceptor in a law office that more than likely was controlled by lawyers of Irish or German descent, or by "old Americans." [28]

Finally, there was the emergence of the automobile accident injury field after World War I. This new type of law business fell primarily into the hands of the metropolitan individual practitioner and soon became one of the most lucrative staples of his practice. Aside from its economic significance, this business had an important impact on the character of the individual lawyer's practice as well. The contingent fee probably first came into prominence with the rise of personal injury practice, and organized solicitation has very likely reached today's dimensions principally because of its use in the personal injury field. Furthermore, the increasing importance of this new field of practice, occurring about the same time the larger firms were taking more and more of the better corporation business matters away from the average practitioner, only widened the gulf between the practice of the elite and the lower-class members of the metropolitan bar.

In comparison with the highly stratified metropolitan bar, the smaller city bar has over the years remained a fairly homogeneous professional community. In social background, professional training,[29] and type of practice, there has been a considerably more limited range of variation among lawyers in the smaller than in the larger city bars. A major reason for this is that the changes we have just been considering, which had the effect of further widening existing class divisions within the metropolitan bar, had considerably less impact on the bar of the smaller cities. Thus there are still no large firms to speak of in these smaller cities;[30] and if there are elites, they apparently have not established exclusive access to the most desirable clients and practice, nor have they restricted entry into their own ranks anywhere near to the same extent as their counterparts have done in the larger cities.

Having considered briefly the route that the individual practitioner takes into the metropolitan bar and the position he occupies in that professional community, we shall now turn to an examination of his work.

NOTES

1. The ethnic composition of the sample of 84 lawyers (see Appendix A, Section 2) is as follows:

TABLE 1

Nationality Background	Per Cent
Northwestern Europe: Britain, Scandinavia, France	8
Ireland	11
Central Europe: Germany, Austria, Czechoslovakia	15
Eastern Europe: Russia, Poland, Lithuania, Romania	53
Southeastern Europe: Italy, Greece, Yugoslavia	5
Africa (Negro)	8
Total	100
Number of cases	(84)

TABLE 2

Religion	Per Cent
Protestant	24
Catholic	21
Jewish	55
Total	100
Number of cases	(84)

TABLE 3

Generation	Per Cent
Foreign born	6
Second generation (at least one parent born abroad)	68
Third generation	13
Fourth or more	13
Total	100
Number of cases	(84)

The class background of the sample is as follows:

TABLE 4

Father's Occupation		Per Cent
Professional		6
Proprietor		63
Manufacturer, processor, wholesaler, jobber	10	
Broker, agent, dealer, independent contractor	20	
Retailer	33	
White-collar (lower managerial, salaried employees, clerical)		19
Blue-collar		12
Total		100
Number of cases		(84)

TABLE 5

Father's Education	Per Cent
College graduate	7
High school graduate	8
Grammar school graduate	25
Some grammar school	17
None, no formal education	43
Total	100
Number of cases	(84)

2. The law school background of the sample is as follows:

TABLE 6

Type of Law School	Per Cent
Full-time University (principally Univ. of Chicago, Univ. of Illinois, and Northwestern Univ.)	33
Part-time and Mixed	
Catholic (DePaul and Loyola)	36
Proprietary (principally Chicago-Kent, John Marshall, and Chicago Law School)	31
Total	100
Number of cases	(84)

The two Catholic law schools are affiliated with Catholic universities, and both have offered a mixed—a morning (full-time) as well as an evening (part-time)—program since the twenties.

The proprietary law schools have no university affiliations and prior to World War II offered only an evening (part-time) program. Chicago-Kent added a morning division in the mid-forties, and John Marshall followed suit in the early fifties. Although most are today incorporated as not-for-profit organizations, these schools have been designated as proprietary since they were generally founded as private profit-making institutions.

Hereafter the term "night law school" will be used to refer to both part-time and mixed law schools.

3. Number of years of college training for respondents from the three types of law schools:

TABLE 7
Type of Law School

Years in College	Full-time University	Catholic	Proprietary	Total
None	4%	0%	31%	11%
One-Two	7	54	35	32
Three	4	13	23	13
Four	85	33	11	44
Total	100%	100%	100%	100%
Number of cases	(28)	(30)	(26)	(84)

4. From the following table it can be seen that in 1923, 4 out of 5 of the night law schools required at best only a high school diploma for admission. Not until the middle thirties did this proportion drop to less than half, and by the early forties to less than 15%. Even as late as 1942, however, there were only 3 night law schools that required more than 2 years of college training for admission.

TABLE 8

Number of College Years Required for Admission	Year					
	1923	*1925*	*1927*	*1934*	*1937*	*1942*
None	80%	68%	58%	55%	34%	14%
One	9	14	15	1	3	0
Two	10	17	26	43	60	82
Three	1	1	1	1	1	1
Four	0	0	0	0	2	3
Total	100%	100%	100%	100%	100%	100%
Number of Night Law Schools	80	92	94	115	99	72

SOURCE: *Annual Review of Legal Education for 1924* (1926, 1928, 1935, 1938), published by the Carnegie Foundation for the Advancement of Teaching (1925–1928), published by the Section of Legal Education and Admission to the Bar of the American Bar Association (1938). See pp. 21, 25, 30, 33, 34–63 of the respective issues. For 1942 figures, *Law School and Bar Admissions Requirements in the U. S. Review of Legal Education.* (Chicago: American Bar Association, Section of Legal Education and Admissions to the Bar, 1942), pp. 3–10.

5. The distribution of law students and law schools by type of law school and whether or not approved by the Council on Legal Education of the American Bar Association for 1932 was as follows:

TABLE 9

Type of Law School	Approved	Not Approved	Total
Full-time			
Students	13,716	1,270	14,986
Schools	73	11	84
Night			
Students	3,989	18,414	22,403
Schools	9	92	101
Total			
Students	17,705	19,684	37,389
Schools	82	103	185

SOURCE: *Annual Review of Legal Education for 1932* (Carnegie Foundation for the Advancement of Teaching, 1933), p. 32.

6. *Annual Review of Legal Education for 1933,* p. 35.

7. Will Shafroth, "Can the Law Schools Lead Us Out of the Wilderness?" *The American Law School Review* (St. Paul, Minn.: West Publishing Co., 1934), VII, 1027–1029. Shafroth had only recently completed a survey of California law schools based on first-hand observation and knew whereof he spoke. See *Report of the California Survey Committee* (Sacramento: State Bar of California, 1933) for a strikingly candid, detailed, and indeed shattering picture of the California night law schools in the thirties. With respect to the selection of students, Shafroth noted:

> A practice analogous to ambulance chasing has grown up where commissions are paid to law students for each new victim they may bring to the school and where solicitors are not only regularly paid to hunt out and sign up prospects but are further compensated as long as their students stay in school. Instances were found where a dean was engaged for a school and was paid a certain amount for each student whom he brought with him or induced to come over from another school (p. 3).

The general character of a substantial proportion of the metropolitan night law schools of that period was well summarized by Shafroth in the same report:

> The weakest type [of law school] is a one-man institution, dominated by a single individual who makes the important decisions and, as a rule, does a large part of the teaching. This kind of school at best has as its highest ambition mere preparation to pass the bar examinations and at its worst the collection of as much money as possible from its students. Usually it is without financial resources, admits any kind of student, whatever his qualifications or lack of them, graduates practically all who remain the required length of time and pay up regularly for their tuition and books, and has only the lowest standards of scholarship. . . . None of them have passed an average of half of their men in the different bar examinations since January, 1929. In some of these institutions the average of success for those taking the bar examinations for the first time has run as low as 20 per cent (p. 2).

For an excellent summary of law school conditions prior to the thirties see Alfred Z. Reed, *Training for the Public Profession of the Law* (New York: Bulletin No. 15 of the Carnegie Foundation for the Advancement of Teaching, 1921), and *Present Day Law Schools in the United States and Canada* (New York: Carnegie Foundation for the Advancement of Teaching, 1928). Reed, who along with Shafroth had alerted the profession to the serious shortcomings of a large proportion of American law schools, was editor of the *Annual Review of Legal Education* which published not only annual statistical data on law schools but also highly informative articles on various phases of legal education.

A follow-up survey of California law schools was published in 1949 under the title *Legal Education and Admissions to the Bar of California* (Sacramento: State Bar of California, 1949). This later study suggests that, while some improvement had been made in the Catholic law schools, the proprietary night law schools remained relatively unchanged. Note the following comment with respect to one of the schools of the latter type:

> This school is deficient as an educational institution, whether judged by entrance requirements, scholastic standards, faculty, administration, physical plant, library or the success of its graduates in the California bar examinations (35.2% successes for graduates of the school taking the exam for the first time between 1932 and 1949). However well intentioned and sincere its dean and faculty, the school is not providing legal education of a quality to justify its tuition fees. It should not continue in operation on its present basis, nor is there any reasonable probability of such improvement as would justify its continuance (p. 223).

That these deplorable conditions continue to exist in many law schools across the country is critically noted in the following articles: Elliott E. Cheatham, "The Law Schools of Tennessee," *Tennessee Law Review*, Vol. XXI (April, 1950); John G. Hervey, "The Decline of Professionalism in the Law: An Exploration into Some Causes," *New York Law Forum*, Vol. III, No. 4 (October, 1957); and John W. Morland, "Legal Education in Georgia," *Mercer Law Review*, Vol. II, No. 2 (Spring, 1951). The Cheatham and Morland articles report on studies conducted for the Survey of the Legal Profession. Substantially better conditions were found in the Pennsylvania law schools in a study conducted for the Survey by Lon Fuller. See Lon L. Fuller, "Legal Education and Admissions to the Bar of Pennsylvania," *Temple Law Quarterly,* XXV, No. 25 (January, 1952).

In this general area, see also Albert J. Harno, *Legal Education in the United States* (San Francisco: Bancroft-Whitney Co., 1952); Joseph T. Tinelly, *Part-Time Legal Education* (Brooklyn, N.Y.: The Foundation Press, 1957); and Lowell S. Nicholson, *The Law Schools of the United States* (Baltimore: Lord Baltimore Press, Inc., 1958). Esther L. Brown, *Lawyers and the Promotion of Justice* (New York: Russell Sage Foundation, 1938) and James Willard Hurst, *The Growth of American Law* (Boston: Little, Brown and Company, 1950) contain valuable sections on legal education, and the findings of the Survey of the Legal Profession with respect to legal education are summarized in Albert P. Blaustein and Charles O. Porter, *The American Lawyer* (Chicago: University of Chicago Press, 1954).

8. *Report of the California Survey Committee* (Sacramento: State Bar of California, 1933), p. 143.

9. Fifty-six per cent of the respondents started out working for other individual or small firm lawyers; two out of three have worked or are now working for such lawyers—better than three out of four, if we include those who clerked for other lawyers while in law school. For a systematic account of the different types of beginning careers followed by young lawyers in Chicago, and the problems which these lawyers face in their first years in practice, see Dan C. Lortie, "The Striving Young Lawyer: A Study of Early Career Differentiation in the Chicago Bar" (unpublished Ph.D. dissertation, University of Chicago, 1958), and "Laymen to Lawmen: Law School, Careers, and Professional Socialization," *Harvard Educational Review,* XXIX, No. 4 (1959), 352–369.

10. Starting salaries for those going into practice before the Depression began at about $5 a week. During the Depression (when most of the respondents were getting started) salaries ranged between $5 and $15 a week. According to one respondent, however: "Fifteen dollars was a lot of money in those days. The ——— firm had a list of 170 men who were willing to work for nothing." During World War II salaries ranged between $25 and $45 a week, and since have climbed to between $55 and $60 a week. These figures are based on reports

from several respondents, and are offered, in the absence of any
statistics on the matter, only as an indication of the general range of
salaries for these various periods.

11.

TABLE 10

DISTRIBUTION OF LAWYERS IN THE UNITED STATES BY
STATUS IN PRACTICE AND CITY SIZE, 1958

Status in Practice	*City Size*				
	Over *500,000*	*200,000–* *500,000*	*50,000–* *200,000*	*Under* *50,000*	*Total* *U.S.*
Individual practitioners	52%	48%	48%	56%	52%
Lawyers in firms	26	24	32	28	28
Lawyers not in private practice (house counsel, govt. legal dept., etc.)	22	28	20	16	20
Total	100%	100%	100%	100%	100%
Number of lawyers	(91,239)	(33,001)	(38,607)	(72,936)	(235,783)

SOURCE: 1958 Supplement to *Lawyers in the United States: Distribution and
Income* (Chicago: American Bar Foundation, 1959), pp. 54–55.

Between 1940 and 1958 there was only a 7 per cent decline in the proportion of individual practitioners in the Chicago bar: 60 per cent of the lawyers listed in *Martindale-Hubbell Law Directory* in 1940 were individual
practitioners; 60% in 1949; and 53% in 1958.

12. How close the biggest New York firms have come to realizing
this ideal may be gathered from the fact that in two of the most
prominent New York firms—Cravath, Swain and Moore, and Sullivan and Cromwell—roughly 90% of the partners are Harvard, Yale,
or Columbia Law School graduates. It is not true, however, that in
hiring young associates these firms take only the graduates of these
three schools, but graduates of other law schools are only rarely made
partners. Thus, of the associates who entered the Cravath firm between 1931 and 1948, 45% were *not* graduates of Harvard, Yale, or
Columbia, and 10% were graduates of night law schools; of those who

subsequently became partners, however, none were from the night schools and close to 70% were Ivy League law school graduates, i.e., of Harvard, Yale, and Columbia. Statistics on the Cravath firm drawn from biographical sketches in Robert T. Swaine, *The Cravath Firm* (New York: Ad Press, Ltd., 1948), Vol. III. Statistics on the Sullivan and Cromwell firm are from Arthur H. Dean, *William Nelson Cromwell* (New York: Ad Press, Ltd., 1957). For a general discussion of the hiring policies of the large New York law firms see Erwin O. Smigel, "The Impact of Recruitment on the Organization of the Large Law Firm," *American Sociological Review*, XXV, No. 1 (1960), 55–66.

That academic achievement is also a prime consideration in the selection of recruits to the large New York firms is supported by the following statistics reported by Smigel:

> The breakdown of the job activities since graduation of the Yale Law School graduating classes for 1955, 1956, and 1957 . . . reveal that 53 per cent of the Yale men the large firms [with 50 or more lawyers] in New York City employed came from the top quarter of their classes, and that 27 per cent were from the first decile (p. 56).

13. The law school background of lawyers in firms with over 25 lawyers in these seven cities is as follows:

TABLE 11

Law School	Chicago	New York	Boston	Phila- delphia	Cleve- land	San Fran- cisco	Los Angeles
Ivy League:							
Harvard	21%	32%	82%	20%	32%	29%	28%
Yale	3	16	4	3	11	5	8
Columbia	1	26	1	1	3	2	1
Total	25	74*	87*	24	46	36	37
Other full-time university	60	12	8	64	51	54	54
Night	15	14	5	12	3	10	9
Total	100%	100%	100%	100%	100%	100%	100%

* The top local law school in this city is an Ivy League law school.

Law School	Chicago	New York	Boston	Phila-delphia	Cleve-land	San Fran-cisco	Los Angeles
No. of lawyers	(581)	(70)	(232)	(361)	(244)	(167)	(166)
No. of firms	16	..	7	10	5	5	4

SOURCE: *Martindale-Hubbell Law Directory* (Summit, N.J.: Martindale-Hubbell, Inc., 1958), Vols. I and II. For all cities except New York, figures are based on total listings in biographical section. Since similar listings are not available for the larger New York City firms, these figures are based on information obtained in my current survey of New York City lawyers (based upon a random sample drawn from the alphabetical listings in the 1960 *Martindale* directory).

14. The law school background of individual practitioners in these seven cities is as follows:

TABLE 12

Law School	Chicago	New York	Boston	Phila-delphia	Cleve-land	San Fran-cisco	Los Angeles
Ivy League	2%	27%	35%	5%	4%	3%	8%
Other full-time universities	29	3	23	45	54	59	42
Night	69	70	42	50	42	38	50
Total	100%	100%	100%	100%	100%	100%	100%
No. of lawyers	(109)	(103)	(79)	(75)	(70)	(65)	(119)

SOURCE: Same as for Table 11 in note 13. Figures for all cities based on random samples drawn from the alphabetical listings in the directory.

15. In Chicago only 10% of the respondents had been an associate in a large firm, held a fairly responsible house counsel or government post, or some combination of these positions.

16. The following table showing the relationship between size of firm and type of law school attended for lawyers in Chicago in private practice suggests that at least as to recruitment there is a fairly distinct middle segment of the metropolitan bar comprised of lawyers in firms with 10 to 25 lawyers. It should be noted also that even

in the small firms lawyers from full-time university law schools begin to outnumber those from night law schools.

TABLE 13

Type of Law School	Individual Practitioners	Lawyers in Firms Size of Firm				
		Small			Middle	Large
		2	3	4–9	10–25	26+
Ivy League	1%	3%	5%	3%	18%	31%
Other full-time university	32	39	45	50	55	54
Night	67	58	50	47	27	15
Total	100%	100%	100%	100%	100%	100%
No. of lawyers	(84)	(38)	(20)	(34)	(74)	(383)

SOURCE: Figures for individual practitioners based on sample in this study; for lawyers in firms of 2 to 9 lawyers, a random sample drawn from *Sullivan's Law Directory for the State of Illinois* (Chicago: Sullivan's Law Directory, 1956), and checked against *Martindale*, 1956, for law school attended; for lawyers in firms of 10 to 25 lawyers, a random sample from *Martindale*, 1956, biographical section; for lawyers in firms of 26 and more lawyers, all lawyers listed in biographical section of *Martindale*, 1956.

17. Hurst characterizes the law firm of the nineteenth century in the following terms:

> From the first quarter of the nineteenth century on, there were partnerships. But no firms of large membership appeared, even in the great cities, until the end of the century. The typical partnership was a two-man affair; it usually had its "office" member and its "court" member; and it ordinarily operated without a formal agreement of partnership, or under an agreement of the simplest kind (James Willard Hurst, *op. cit.*, p. 306).

Koegel reports that in 1872 only one law firm in New York City was listed in *Hubbell's Legal Directory* with as many as 6 partners; and in 1900 only 2 with as many as 9 partners. Otto E. Koegel, *Walter S. Carter, Collector of Young Masters* (Great Neck, N.Y.: Round Table Press, 1955), p. 7.

18. Some indication of the rapid growth of the large firm after the

turn of the century may be had from the histories of the New York law firms of Cravath, Swaine and Moore, Sullivan and Cromwell, and Cadwalader, Wickersham and Taft. From 1819 (when the first of a line of firms leading to the present firm was organized) to 1898, none of the predecessor firms of the present Cravath firm had more than five lawyers. During the following eight or ten years the number of lawyers increased to about 30. Thereafter the size of the firm remained relatively constant until 1920. Between 1920 and 1930 the number of lawyers more than doubled (34 to 77) and between 1930 and 1940 there was better than a 50% increase (77 to 118) (Robert T. Swaine, *op. cit.*, Vol. III. Prior to 1920 the Sullivan and Cromwell firm increased at a more even rate than the Cravath firm (from 5 lawyers in 1880 to 7 in 1890, 14 in 1900, 21 in 1910, and 32 in 1920); then, like the Cravath firm, it almost doubled in size during the twenties (from 32 to 60 lawyers). Since 1930, however, the Sullivan firm has increased at a slower pace than Cravath (76 lawyers in 1940 and 90 in 1950) (Arthur H. Dean, *op. cit.*). Data on the Cadwalader firm is less complete but the same pattern of growth was in evidence. The predecessor firm of Strong and Cadwalader started with 6 lawyers in 1878, and when the present firm was constituted in 1914 had increased to 23 lawyers. The next figure which we have, 62 lawyers in 1938, suggests a similar rapid rise during the twenties. Henry W. Taft, *A Century and a Half at the New York Bar* (New York: Privately printed, 1938).

19. "When Cravath entered [the Seward firm] as a partner in 1899 he brought to the firm a philosophy of organization quite different from that which had previously prevailed in the Blatchford and Seward firms [predecessors of the present Cravath firm]. That philosophy, of which he himself was a product, had been developed by Walter S. Carter, whose office Cravath had entered when he graduated from Columbia Law School. It was Carter's practice to seek, annually, one or more of the best graduates of the leading law schools, principally Columbia, and train them through a clerkship of several years" (Robert T. Swaine, *op. cit.*, I, 3). According to Swaine, the high scholastic standards of the "Cravath system" were, in 1899, "regarded as somewhat eccentric—not to say stuffy." It could not have taken too many years, however, before such standards were adopted by most newly emerging larger firms, many of the leading members of which, like Cravath, had been "graduates" of the Carter office (see Koegel, *op. cit.*, pp. 102–111).

20. Robert T. Swaine, *op. cit.,* Vol. III.

21. Arthur H. Dean, *op. cit.,* p. i.

22. Practically to the end of the nineteenth century most lawyers entered the practice of law (in the larger as well as the smaller cities) after a period of apprenticeship in an older lawyer's office. By 1920 this system of law office apprenticeship had been virtually replaced by a formal period of training in a law school. Thus of the 22,859 persons who took the New York State bar examination in the decade from 1922 to 1931 (inclusive) only 193 were law office trained, or less than 1%. Philip J. Wickser, "Law Schools, Bar Examiners, and Bar Associations—Co-operation vs. Insulation," *American Law School Review,* VII (1933), 729. While further research is needed to document the exact period when this change occurred, it appears that the principal shift took place between 1890 and 1910.

23. Two factors in particular were responsible for this sudden transformation in professional training. The first was the introduction of formal written examinations in the 1890's as part of a general effort at tightening bar admissions requirements. This reform was apparently effected in a single decade: "Before 1890 only four states had boards of bar examiners, and in no more than half a dozen had written examinations been used. However, when the leading law schools began to use the written examinations, this encouraged adoption of the practice in the states, where it became the invariable method of examination after 1900" (Hurst, *op. cit.,* p. 283). That the introduction of written bar examinations did not contribute to raising educational standards was regretfully conceded by Reed in 1921: ". . . there can be little question but that, in spite of all recent efforts to raise bar examination standards, more incompetents are today admitted to the bar than when, under laxer formal requirements for admission and a smaller development of good law schools than we now possess, the generality of actual applicants nevertheless received a sound training in the office of an old fashioned practitioner" (*Training for the Public Profession of Law,* p. 59). What Reed failed to recognize was that there were more incompetents very likely *because* of the efforts to raise bar examination standards in so far as this stimulated the development of the night law school. Whatever the educational advantages of a law office apprenticeship, systematic preparation for an academic examination was certainly not one of them. The night law school, on the other hand, whatever its educational disadvantages,

did hold out the promise of—and had as its principal aim—preparation for the state bar examination. Ironically, then, one may in part attribute the rise of the night law school with its notoriously low educational standards to a reform movement that had as its goal the raising of educational standards for admission to practice.

The second factor that contributed to the rise of the night law school was the advent (also around the turn of the century) of the typewriter, which led to the substitution of the "stenographer for the longhand copyist . . . [which in turn] brought a gradual, but in the long run, very substantial decrease in the law offices' demand for student clerks" (Hurst, *op. cit.*, p. 257). Another invention, the electric light, should probably also be included in this list of factors: ". . . with improvements in methods of artificial illumination it became possible finally to hold sessions in the evening, thereby extending the opportunities to secure a legal education to a still wider element of the population" (Reed, *Training for the Public Profession of Law*, p. 56).

24.

TABLE 14

CHANGES IN THE LAWYER POPULATION OF
THE UNITED STATES, 1900–1958

Year	Number of Lawyers	Per Cent Increase Over Previous Date
1900	109,140	..
1910	114,704	6
1920	122,519	8
1930	160,605	31
1940	180,483	12
1950	204,111	13
1958	235,783	15

SOURCE: U.S. Census, *Statistical Abstract of the United States for 1900–1950;* 1958 Supplement to Lawyers in the United States: *Distribution and Income,* for 1958 figure.

25. In 1920 there were 25,120 lawyers in the ten largest cities (New York, Chicago, Philadelphia, Detroit, Cleveland, St. Louis, Boston, Baltimore, Pittsburgh, and Los Angeles); in 1930 there were 38,596. These statistics were compiled from Fourteenth Census of the U.S.,

Vol. IV, *Population,* 1930, and Fifteenth Census of the U.S., Vol. IV, *Population,* 1930.

26. Between 1920 and 1929 the number of law students enrolled in law schools located in cities of 200,000 or more population more than doubled (114% increase). Most of this increase was accounted for by the night law schools, which increased 142% compared to 47% for the full-time law schools (*Annual Review of Legal Education for 1921–1930*). In 1928, the year of peak law school enrollment prior to World War II, 4 out of 5 law students in cities with over a half million population were in night law schools, and 1 out of 3 of *all* law students in the United States were located in just 10 night law schools situated in or near Boston and New York (*Annual Review of Legal Education for 1932,* pp. 29–33). That most of these graduates became individual practitioners is evident from Table 11 in note 13.

27. Some indication of this shift may be had from the following statistics for the New York City bar:

(1) In 1900, of all foreign-born and second-generation lawyers (most of whom presumably were individual practitioners) in New York City, approximately 65% were of Irish or Central European origin (Twelfth Census of the United States, Vol. IV, *Population,* 1900), compared to about 25% today (Columbia University Metropolitan Law Office Study, in progress).

(2) The proportion of Jewish lawyers entering the New York City bar from the turn of the century to the mid-thirties increased from 26% to 80%:

TABLE 15

PROPORTION OF JEWISH LAWYERS ENTERING THE
NEW YORK CITY BAR, 1900–1934

Lawyers Admitted to Practice	Per Cent Jewish	Number of Cases
1900–1910	26	(623)
1911–1917	36	(491)
1918–1923	40	(566)
1924–1929	56	(1,501)
1930–1934	80	(1,382)

SOURCE: Compiled from figures presented in Melvin J. Fagen, "The Status of Jewish Lawyers in New York City," *Jewish Social Studies,* I, 1939, 73–104.

The increase in the proportion of foreign-born and second-generation lawyers in the metropolitan bar apparently occurred at a somewhat slower rate. In New York City, for example, 47% of the bar was first or second generation in 1900, 53% in 1910, 55% in 1920, and 69% today (Twelfth-Fourteenth Census of the United States, Vol. IV, *Population*, 1900–1920; Metropolitan Law Office Study).

28. Indirect support for this conclusion may be found in Fuller's assessment of the Pennsylvania preceptorship system under which a prospective law student must obtain an "acceptable preceptor before he begins his law studies." Lon Fuller (*op. cit.*, pp. 289–290) notes:

> When the system of preceptorships was installed in 1928, some students for a time had difficulty in obtaining preceptors. . . . Shortly after the system was announced there was a large meeting of Jewish lawyers in Philadelphia who pledged themselves that no worthy and able Jewish student should be denied registration as a law student because of inability to obtain a preceptor. . . . The incident tends to show that under the Pennsylvania system elements of discrimination manifest themselves . . . before the student has even entered law school. Naturally at this point tendencies to discrimination are likely to be at their height. There is nothing to counteract them. The prospective employer who can only guess at the legal ability of his prospective clerk will tend to prefer those of a religious and cultural background similar to his own.

29. In five cities in Iowa with populations of 45,000 to 178,000, 93% of the lawyers are full-time university law school graduates, over 70% from just two law schools, the State University of Iowa and Drake University. In five cities in Illinois, with populations of 40,000 to 100,000, 70% are graduates of full-time university law schools, 35% from the University of Illinois (compiled from *Martindale*, Vol. I, 1958). In the northeastern states, because of the proximity of both Ivy League and night law schools and the absence of any state university law schools, we find more variation in law school background among lawyers in the smaller cities.

30. In an examination of *Martindale* (Vol. I, 1958) I found no firms with as many as 15 lawyers in cities of less than 200,000 population, and very few with more than 5 or 6 lawyers. In Des Moines, Iowa, for example, with a population of approximately 178,000, and

a bar of 623 lawyers, the largest firm has only 10 lawyers, and there are only 8 firms with over 6 lawyers. In Rockford, Ill., with a population of approximately 105,000 and a bar of 157 lawyers, the largest firm has only 7 lawyers, and there are only 4 firms with more than 4 lawyers.

2

The Work of the
Individual Practitioner

A Loop law office occupied on a rent-sharing basis with two or three other lawyers is the principal work setting of most individual practitioners in Chicago.[1] The individual lawyer is in his office an average of four to five hours a day conferring with clients and handling office paper work.[2] A little over an hour a day will be spent in court, generally in the clerk's office of one of the county or municipal courts filing documents or answering court calls.[3] Another hour a day is spent in the administrative agencies of government, and here again it is the city and county agencies that claim the largest share of the lawyer's time.[4] The remainder of his day may be occupied with a visit to a title company, a client's place of business, a law library, the office of a bank or trust company, insurance or real estate agent, or a savings and loan association.

The work of the individual practitioner will be described in terms of what the respondents are doing in each of eight areas of practice—business-corporate, real estate, tax, personal injury, divorce, will-probate-estate, criminal, and collections.[5]

A distinction will be made here between those respondents whose practice consists largely of a bookkeeping operation, seldom going beyond the filling in of a standard form or a routine appearance before a court or agency—who will be referred to as lower-level lawyers—and respondents whose practice almost invariably involves the exercise of a higher level of technical skill—who will be referred to as upper-level lawyers.

BUSINESS-CORPORATE

A business organization frequently encounters problems requiring specialized help, particularly in its dealings with outside agencies that impinge upon or restrict its operations. Thus, at its inception, the corporation must meet certain requirements set up by the state before being licensed to operate. Later, if the corporation wants to change its structure or dissolve itself, it must also follow certain prescribed forms and procedures. Furthermore, there are certain requirements placed upon it by various taxing bodies and other governmental agencies—labor departments, zoning boards, building departments, and so on—at the local, state, and federal levels. This means that there are documents or forms that must be filled out, filed, and recorded according to prescribed rules. Beyond this it means that the corporation's policies and operations, and whatever agreements it may enter into, must be considered in the light of various regulations and standards. There may be occasions when these regulations and standards are not met—when the corporation finds it necessary to defend itself or to make certain appeals to these bodies. Likewise, in dealing with employees or their union agents, in meeting problems of financing, and in the numerous transactions of purchase or sale, there are documents to be prepared or executed, agencies to be dealt with, rules to be followed, and technical pitfalls to be avoided, all of which may require specialized assistance. Such assistance may be provided by accountants, tax advisers, management consultants, bank or investment company officials, public relations experts, politicians, and, of course, by lawyers.

The minimal functions that individual lawyers are called upon to perform for their business clients include incorporation, preparation of minutes of stockholders' and directors' meetings, and routine filings.

The incorporation of a small business is in most cases a routine matter for which a flat fee is charged and involves: (1) drawing up the articles of incorporation, which generally means filling in a standard form; (2) delivering the articles to the Secretary of State and filing the duplicate and a certificate of incorporation with the County Recorder of Deeds; and (3) preparing the minutes of the first meeting of the corporation's stockholders and directors (for which there is also a form).[6]

As secretary of the corporation the lawyer will often prepare the pro forma minutes of subsequent meetings, which are usually not attended by the individuals in question but are merely designed to meet the legal requirements of the state of incorporation.

"Routine filing" refers to various documents that have

to be prepared and filed more or less regularly for a business concern. These may include: (1) the annual report to the Secretary of State, made out on forms prescribed by his office; (2) the state franchise, property and sales tax returns, and unemployment compensation payments and reports to the State Director of Labor; (3) the federal corporate income tax returns, social security payments, and employees' federal withholding tax forms.

In addition, most individual lawyers prepare leases and stock purchase contracts, look after building and zoning violations, handle personal matters both for employees and for the officers and directors of the corporation, provide general business advice, and occasionally handle a labor relations problem or a case in litigation.

These, then, are the minimal tasks that the individual lawyer is called upon to perform for his corporate client. In most cases these are fairly specific jobs of a routine, highly standardized character, many of which may be handled by the small businessman himself or by his secretary, bookkeeper, accountant, or auditor. As was pointed out:

> They generally run their own business, except when they get into difficulty—a bad contract—they might have a contract thing, or a zoning law, a violation of the code. (89)

> Their accountant does most of this routine stuff. (76)

The practice of about half the individual practitioners specializing (that is, with 30 per cent or more of their practice) in the business-corporate area is confined to the intermittent performance of these lower-level tasks for their small, generally neighborhood, business clients.

Most of the time of the lower-level business-corporate

lawyers is spent in the preparation and filing of routine documents and consulting with clients—often at their place of business. Contact with government agencies is generally limited to local or state agencies—principally the Secretary of State's Office, the County Recorder's Office, and the local tax and zoning boards. Only two lower-level practitioners mentioned that they had any contact with a federal agency: one with the War Labor Board during World War II, and the other occasionally represented a client before the National Labor Relations Board.

Some time is also spent with accountants, who may be either in the direct employ of the client or in an independent firm whose services are utilized by the client.

The accountant appears to be the most serious competitor of the business-corporate lawyer, particularly of the lower-level practitioner. Many of the latter, for example, complained that accountants draw up corporate resolutions and minutes of directors' meetings, and one very bitterly noted that accountants often wean clients away from lawyers and frequently displace the lawyer in the affection and regard of the client:

> Accountants have the faculty of ingratiating themselves with clients to a greater degree than lawyers. They have an "in" through keeping their books, and so on. Clients will tell me, "I've discussed it with my accountant," oftentimes referring to a matter they should have discussed with a lawyer. (18)

In view of the intermittent character of the work involved and the economically marginal position of most of their business clients, it is not surprising to find that the relationship of the lower-level lawyer to his business clients is often less secure than he would like it to be. In answer to the question of whether he had any permanent clients one lower-level respondent noted, for example:

> It's hard to say percentage-wise. You know it's very diffi-cult—the ordinary lawyer figures probably if he represents a business he gets all of their business. But you can't always be sure. (24)

Another replied:

> How do you call any client permanent? I had one for seven years, the son becomes a lawyer, or the daughter marries into a family where there are lawyers—I wouldn't call any client permanent. (76)

The remaining specialists in this area, the upper-level practitioners, provide a more continuous and less periph-eral type of service for their larger business clients and are more intimately involved in a wider range of their clients' problems.

An indication of the wider range of activities engaged in by upper-level lawyers may be gathered from the follow-ing workday account:

> Instead of coming downtown I went to the client's office. There I handled a tax matter [personal property tax], a labor management matter [a grievance matter with the shop committee], an insurance matter [payment of a loss], and another insurance matter relating to revision of fire rates, and I had to consult with the plant superintendent relating to a policy of operations. I also had to process a garnishment relating to one of the employees—that's one of the services I perform for the employees. Then there was another insurance matter—the cancellation of an insurance policy of one of its contractors who left for Puerto Rico. . . . When I got back to the office I went through my mail,

dictated a letter to a client informing him of a decision
of a board of review—a determination of a referee for
the Unemployment Compensation Board. . . . Before you
came I was working on a franchise agreement for a client
. . . licensing firms, permitting them to use the registered
name of my client. Then I worked on a lease with the Con-
tainer Corporation—and when you came I was in the process of co-ordinating the corporate minutes with the franchise agreement. I may remain here this evening to work
on a stock liquidation program for a client. (15)

There are four areas of activities that lower-level practitioners engage in either only occasionally or not at all
that figure prominently in the practice of upper-level business-corporate lawyers: general business advice, handling
labor relations problems, contract matters, and corporate
financing.

Nearly all the upper-level practitioners said they provided general business advice for their clients. Typical
of the comments in this regard are the following: "I sit in
on planning and all vital concerns"; "I'm in on business
consultations—I advise on business policy. I'm a member
of the board for several"; "I give analysis and advice on oil
deals"; "I'm at directors' meetings and advise them; in
many I act as director—mainly I sit in an advisory capacity
with directors and officers."

A good number mentioned handling labor problems,
mostly in the union-management field—grievances, contract renewals, organizing efforts. Personnel matters also
are dealt with, including pension plans and the like.

Although contract matters occupy at least a part of the
time for some lower-level practitioners, they were mentioned by all but one of the upper-level lawyers. Not only
are such matters more frequently handled by the latter,

but they tend to be related to more complicated deals involving larger sums of money. One lawyer, for example, on the day prior to our interview, had been in a conference in connection with a deal involving the purchase of a rather sizable business:

> I went out to the yards with one of the corporate clients. We saw some people who wanted to sell a business that was a competitor of ours. It involves analyzing the size of the sellers' business, the quantity of raw materials that they buy, the finished product that they sell, a consideration of fixed assets and annual income. Those present were: the president of my client, the principal owner of the sellers and their financial adviser. The four of us discussed it for four hours. The main reason I was there was because of the antitrust implications of the acquisition—a quarter of a million dollars is involved, and they've been in trouble before. (68)

A number of upper-level lawyers said they handled various phases of corporate financing, an area not mentioned at all by the lower-level lawyers. One upper-level lawyer, for instance, had been spending a great deal of time on the preparation of a public stock issue involving the registration of a corporation in Panama and on a stock liquidation program. Problems of corporate reorganization, merger, and consolidation involving important questions of financing also were mentioned by several of these lawyers.

Consultation with clients and office paper work take up most of the time of the upper- as well as the lower-level business-corporate lawyer. The paper work, however, is generally less routine and more technically demanding than is the case with lower-level lawyers. An upper-level practitioner who devotes a good deal of time to the preparation of documents involving rather complicated transactions gave the following account of this type of work:

> I write it [the document] out at home and then dictate it at the office: checking on easements and remodeling plans, a mechanics' lien foreclosure that I'm defending, details on the consolidation of two corporations, another problem involving a special clause in a large insurance policy with premiums in five figures, another consolidation of corporations. I put in, on the average, at least one to two hours' work every night. I do most of my drafting at home—contracts, corporate minutes, lengthy matters. (85)

Considerable time is spent with accountants. Since the latter are frequently in the possession of essential information on the operation of the business, including of course its books and records, they usually constitute an important link between the client and the upper-level lawyer.

> I work with accountants often. I'm familiar with their procedures, and I discuss clients' problems with them. (50)

Because they have a more permanent and secure relationship to their clients the upper-level lawyers are in a better position to work out a fairly well-defined division of labor between themselves and the accountants and for that reason feel less threatened by the accountants than do the lower-level practitioners. As one upper-level lawyer noted:

> Actually I do not have much cause for complaint—they [accountants] are not a threat. Actually I lean on CPA's—on pension programs, tax consequences, and the like. (15)

Contact with the courts appears to be minimal for upper-level lawyers, but what contact there is is with the federal courts. Considerably more time is spent by these lawyers in governmental agencies, principally the federal agencies in the labor, trade, and security fields. One upper-level lawyer, for example, gave the following account of his dealings with certain federal agencies:

> I'm in Washington with the FTC people once a month—at the same time I usually see the lawyers in the antitrust division. In the labor field I usually come in contact with field examiners and investigators—on elections, eligibility requirements—a couple of hours a week. In Chicago I'm in contact with the Regional Director of the NLRB and their agents and members of the investigating staff—generally over the phone. Occasionally I have contact with the Pure Food and Drug people—in the local office here. On the 11th I went to Washington on a matter—they wanted to put the president of the company in jail—too many frozen eggs went bad. . . . Department of Agriculture—I get into those things too. (68)

This relatively high incidence of contact with federal agencies on the part of upper-level lawyers contrasts sharply not only with the experience of lower-level business-corporate lawyers but also with most others in the sample, whose only contact with federal agencies is likely to be with the local office of the Bureau of Internal Revenue on individual tax matters.

Several upper-level lawyers previously held posts in federal agencies: one respondent, for example, was with the NRA for a short time in the thirties, handling enforcement code problems for retail auto dealers; another was with the OPA in Washington as a senior business analyst, helping to develop price schedules. There can be little doubt that their experiences in these agencies and the contacts they made enhanced their opportunities to attract the larger corporate clients and have enabled them since to deal more effectively with such agencies. The lawyer who had been with the OPA during the war commented:

> Since I'd been in Washington I became known as a specialist in government controls. When I came back I had a volume of government work in the administrative area—wage and hour, labor, war controls, and defense controls—I was on retainer with several defense plants controlling strategic materials—aircraft components—during shortages I expedited acquisitions. With the Taft-Hartley Act my labor practice increased—handling management side only—and corporate trust practice, all heavy stuff, trust contracts, organizations and reorganizations, and the like. (15)

Many more individual practitioners came in contact with federal agencies during World War II than either before or since that time. Controls on rents, prices, wages, and strategic materials often brought the small businessman and small corporation up against problems requiring the special services of a lawyer. Problems in the area of wage controls, for example, provided considerable work for several lawyers in the sample.

> I did a lot of reclassification work—that was my specialty in those days. . . . We'd upgrade jobs so they could pay higher wages. I'd do the job analysis to determine the job grade—that was my specialty. [Respondent still had some of the forms and documents he used at that time and showed me one or two job analyses he had handled.] I was grossing as much as $10,000 a month then. (12)

REAL ESTATE

The most frequently dealt with matter coming under the general heading of real estate is the residential closing. What is involved in such a closing? What tasks are the lawyers called upon to perform?

The "closing" is a term applied to the consummation of a real estate transaction, at which time the seller conveys title to the property in question in return for the buyer's tendering of the purchase price.

The first step leading to the closing (after the preliminary negotiations) is the execution of a purchase agreement between buyer and seller. This will generally be written into a standardized form contract and will usually contain a provision that the agreement is subject to the seller's obtaining a title guarantee policy (or an acceptable opinion letter from the title company) and the buyer's success in procuring a loan (usually a first mortgage loan).

In the next step the buyer makes application for a mortgage at a lending institution, generally a savings and loan association in the type of transaction with which we are concerned here. The buyer signs the necessary notes and mortgage papers, which are then recorded at the County Recorder's Office by the loan association. At about the same time the seller, or someone acting on his behalf, will make application to the title company for an owner's title guarantee policy.[7] That agency will make a title search on the basis of which it will send a formal opinion letter stating "objections," that is, listing whatever outstanding claims, unpaid judgments, tax liens, mortgage liens, etc., there may be against the property. Upon instructions from the seller the title company will then issue a guarantee policy to the buyer (with whatever objections still remain)—the seller generally paying the fees. Once these matters have been taken care of, the closing can follow.[8]

The closing itself will generally occur at the savings and loan association, but may take place at the title company, the real estate broker's office, or at the lawyer's office. At the closing the seller will convey title to the property by means of a deed. This document (like the purchase agreement and mortgage papers) is generally written into a standardized form. The buyer tenders the purchase price in return for the deed. Immediately thereafter the buyer will have the deed recorded at the County Recorder's Office.

In most transactions there will be a real estate broker in the picture. His principal function is to bring together the prospective buyer and seller, and he generally enters the transaction at the initial stage as agent of the seller. He will have all the requisite forms (purchase agreement, application for mortgage, and title guarantee policy, etc.) and will frequently fill them out for the parties. The broker, like the lawyer or the title company, may act as stakeholder, holding the "earnest" money or part of the purchase price in escrow, in which case the closing may be held in his office. Many lawyers, however, insist on having the broker come to their office for the closing and prior negotiations, if that choice is open. Several respondents felt rather strongly about this:

> They [the real estate brokers] call us a louse. They like to close deals there, but I won't go. I *will* go to the Chicago Title and Trust Company.

Interviewer: Why?

Respondent: It's a matter of protocol, I feel. They [the real estate brokers] will sell a house and get a $500 commission, and I'll get $100 if I'm lucky—and I do more work. (37)

Usually they come here. They're making the commission—for closing and preparing the papers—they come here. (46)

Sometimes the real estate broker will refer the parties to a lawyer with whom he is associated. Furthermore, it is not uncommon for a neighborhood real estate broker to have a lawyer right in his office—and in some instances the real estate broker may himself be a lawyer. More often than not, however, the real estate broker views the lawyer as a competitor, and according to many respondents will discourage the parties from seeking legal representation. The lawyer considers the real estate broker to be his most serious competitor in the real estate field. The usual complaint is that real estate brokers prepare documents (purchase contracts, deeds) and close deals, in addition to advising clients that they need not seek a lawyer's assistance:

Real estate brokers are serious competitors, and they have the active co-operation of the Chicago Title and Trust Company. They prepare contracts of sale of real property—generally handle the deal from beginning to end.

Interviewer: Does that hurt you?

Respondent: My real estate business would pick up twentyfold. (28)

The keenest competition is from real estate brokers and accountants; they have invaded the law field tremendously.

Real estate brokers have taken a great deal of the small real estate closings. (18)

Most real estate brokers tell them [clients] that they don't need a lawyer. (19)

Most closings on small residential properties appear to be held at the offices of a savings and loan association. Partly because of its appeal to neighborhood ethnic groups, and its connections with local real estate brokers and promoters, and partly because of its greater willingness to advance loans in situations where the banks and insurance companies have been more hesitant, the savings and loan association has become the principal lending institution in most small residential purchases. It is generally in a position to insist on handling most phases of the real estate transaction, including the final closing; and the buyer, because of his inexperience, is usually willing to let the loan association handle the deal.

Next to the real estate broker, the savings and loan association is viewed as the individual lawyer's most serious competitor in handling real estate matters. Many respondents complained rather bitterly of this encroachment:

The savings and loan association, they handle all the details on the loan, the mortgage.
Interviewer: Have you felt it—the competition from the savings and loan association?
Respondent: I'm subject to it. A client buying property called me in, wanted me to represent him, and asked me how much I would charge him. When I told him, he said the loan association will do it for less, and will do all the work. I told him to let the loan association carry through with it. (21)

The savings and loan associations act as lawyers, closing deals—they don't say go out and hire a lawyer, but they give it to a closing flunky who gets a $100 a week. (30)

There is a loss of business from the savings and loan associations where they close deals and charge a fee for drawing a mortgage. They say, "We can look after the papers, you don't need a lawyer." They take some real estate law work from us. (8)

Clients tell me of a house they've already bought, they come in and ask me to look over the contract. The brokers, the savings and loan associations—it's a miserable situation—they practice law, prepare deeds, and lawyers spend all their time prosecuting them. Savings and loan associations charge a fee for a lawyer, even when the lawyer is their own company lawyer. (45)

Negotiating with real estate brokers and other lawyers, conferring with clients, and participating in closings probably account for the largest portion of the lawyer's time in this area. In addition, a few hours a week may be spent at the title company setting up or checking on an escrow account, depositing documents or cash in escrow, and "clearing objections." Contact with the courts is minimal, and little time is devoted to the preparation of documents. Only one respondent mentioned doing any research in connection with a real estate closing.

It is difficult to say with any certainty what proportion of closings involve the services of a lawyer (other than the lawyer for the real estate promoter or lending institution), but most people with whom I have discussed the problem, including the lawyers in the sample, seem to agree that it is only in a very small proportion of the cases.

In one out of twenty deals people ask for attorneys. If they don't ask, brokers don't want them to have any. They just want their commission. (28)

The lawyer, if he enters the transaction at all, generally does so at the end, merely to look over an accomplished fact or possibly to fill out a standardized form. His role is thus a minor one, at the most mediating between the client and various institutions after most of the technicalities have been ironed out. Thus one lawyer stated when asked about his role in a real estate deal:

I deal mostly with the individual client. There may be a broker in already, and the mortgage may already have been obtained. I meet with the mortgage people—primarily the savings and loan association—more so than the broker. (16)

Another lawyer had been called in at the end of negotiations for the purchase of a three-flat apartment building:

I discussed it with the client. A contract had been prepared and I checked it. I gave it back to the real estate broker for revision. The purchaser is eager to get it. (52)

Of the lawyers specializing in the real estate field, about half are primarily handling residential closings for lower-income, individual clients and may be classified as lower-level practitioners. Most of these lawyers have a neighborhood practice, and all but one rely heavily on particular ethnic groups as a source of clientele. These lawyers, on occasion, also draft leases, iron out squabbles between landlord and tenant, handle rent collections and evictions, and now and then take a condemnation or zoning matter, or a possible building code violation.

In sharp contrast to the practice of these lawyers is the work of the upper-level real estate specialists. The latter, with one or two exceptions, are involved in commercial real estate matters for business or corporate—as opposed to individual—clients. Some are the legal advisers of the real estate developers and promoters. One such lawyer had spent most of the day before our interview ironing out some financing problems for a syndicate of real estate developers.

> At 12:30 I met a couple of clients, real estate developers, and had lunch with them. We came back to the office and were there until 5:00—actually between my office and a mortgage house in this building—straightening out certain loans that they had started processing. The credit of the applicants was questionable because of their inability to earn enough to qualify for a mortgage under the Veterans Administration. We were trying to get an advance of money for [loans] not completed. They checked the files and documents, and we finally got a check for advances to meet the demands of the subcontractors. They left at 5:30. (65)

This respondent defined his real estate practice as falling primarily in the field of land development and federal housing. "The bulk of the work is for corporations buying raw land and manufacturing it into completed homes. We sell mostly to veterans under FHA- and VA-guaranteed loans. We get loans through mortgage houses that act as our broker or we get the lender to give us intermediate financing." (65)

Another lawyer had a corporate client planning an expansion of its industrial property that raised a number of problems he was just going into at the time I interviewed him:

> Yesterday I worked on a real estate matter—industrial land—for a corporation that is adding on to what it now has. I was checking the property—it has all kinds of restrictions and easements—it's involved. I have to look over opinion letters from the Chicago Title and Trust Company, land tracts, railroad rights; it's not like buying an apartment building. I went over the letter, checked maps and surveys—I'll spend the rest of the week on just that. (46)

A large real estate deal was the current interest of another upper-level respondent:

> I was working on a $200,000 real estate deal, drawing up a contract, agreement—had to make a lot of telephone calls—both parties were here. It's a multiple dwelling—a business deal, in which I represent the buyers. The sellers are real estate brokers. Afterwards the clients came to my house, where we talked business—we worked from nine to two in the morning. I also worked on an agreement obtaining a waiver on a building costing $400,000 in the Loop. I get a lot of piddling deals, but yesterday, you asked me—what a day! (50)

The functions performed by upper-level real estate lawyers are far less peripheral and require a greater degree of technical skill than the functions performed by lawyers handling residential closings. The upper-level lawyers are not coming in at the end of a deal; on the contrary, they provide more or less continuous legal service for permanent clients who are either in the business of buying and selling real estate or who get into real estate transactions in the course of other business activities. The deals they handle, furthermore, are too large and too complicated to be treated on a purely routine, standardized basis, and far more time therefore is given to preparation of documents and paper work by upper-level lawyers than by lower-level lawyers.

A number of real estate practitioners, starting from circumstances similar to those of the lower-level lawyers, managed to move beyond the narrow confines of this type of practice and in time, as they became more and more involved in their own as well as their clients' real estate ventures, moved out of the practice of law altogether. One such lawyer described this process in some detail. Note also in his reminiscences the successive phases of real estate practice in Chicago from the twenties on, and the way in which the ethnic real estate lawyer, along with others in the real estate field, facilitated the geographic and social mobility of the original inhabitants of the ethnic islands in the city:

> In 1923 I went to work for ———. He had a large real estate practice, a terrific real estate practice. In the twenties there was a terrific building boom, a lot of Jews on the West Side went into the building business. He represented hosts of them on the West Side; they were building up the Lawndale district, Jewish real estate men, builders and contractors—very active. Not many Jewish lawyers handled that business. The German-Jewish lawyers [specifying a prominent firm]—they didn't do that. There were about twenty lawyers who did the work. . . . I did all the work, he didn't even know how to dictate a letter in good English. He started speculating in Florida—the building boom there, and his practice devolved on me. He was advancing my salary, and then we formed a partnership

which lasted until 1930. In 1930 the Depression hit him—
he did a terrific business in second mortgages. When he
lost everything, he became impossible. I've been practicing
alone ever since—he cured me of ever wanting a partner.
. . . During the thirties there were a lot of foreclosures,
but we run-of-the-mill lawyers didn't get 'em, but ———
and ——— [two firms] did. One represented the receivers,
the other the other side. They [these two firms] had it
sewed up pretty well. They speak of the bankruptcy ring
of half a dozen firms that work together, it's like that. But
we had considerable foreclosure work, and chancery work
of various types—a lot of clients. I began to represent men
who were leasing and buying hotels—if you had money in
those days you could get terrific bargains. While representing these people in the thirties I learned about the
hotel business and about investments. I had some money
in, but I lost up to that time—I wasn't too lucky. In 1941,
late in 1941, there was a real estate broker I was active
with, he suggested I go to Kansas City and look at various
properties there that several insurance companies owned,
through foreclosures. Their period was later than ours. In
1941 in Chicago the situation was cleaned up and we were
going ahead, rents were going up, we were coming out of
the depression. In Kansas City they were still in it, rents
were the lowest in any large city—you could buy 'em
cheaper. We went there and found that you could buy
real estate with 10 per cent down and low figures. We
knew—Truman was senator—it was bound to get a lot of
government business brought in by the war. We invested,
the broker and myself, we just put up deposits—that was
all we had—and we came back and got all our friends to
invest with us. Sometimes we got a percentage of the deal
for bringing the business. . . . We gave up our apartment in Chicago. My wife is quite a businesswoman—we
had about ten apartment hotel buildings—and she super-

vised the managers of our properties. Truman brought government business to Kansas City, and it became a boom town. . . . In 1946 we came back [to Chicago]. . . . In the meantime my partner and I bought this building [a Near North Side hotel], and in 1949 I moved my office here. . . . In the twenties I was representing builders, property owners, traders in real estate; in the thirties, chancery work, mostly foreclosures; in the forties I was representing real estate people generally. Then I began to make these investments, and coming out here my law practice suffered considerably. But I get more probate work with money. Couple of years back one of my [business] partners died leaving an $800,000 estate. Handling that gave me a damn nice fee! . . . I'd say that 25 per cent of my time now is devoted to my law practice. (40)

TAX

For those lawyers who handle more than just an occasional tax matter the most commonly dealt with problem is the real estate tax foreclosure. The relatively high incidence of tax foreclosure work in Chicago is related to the rapid expansion since World War II of new residential construction on the periphery of the city, utilizing land that heretofore has either been vacant or used for other purposes. A large proportion of these properties have for years been burdened with unpaid taxes, many with delinquent taxes and unpaid assessments going back to the late twenties. Since the real estate market was generally inactive in the intervening period, little serious attention was given to this problem until after the war. In the thirties, however, some attempts were made to set up machinery to bring these properties back on the tax rolls of the county, and by the end of the thirties there were statutory provisions that enabled the county to foreclose on tax delinquent property giving the subsequent buyers relatively clear title.[9] The present tax foreclosure procedures are handled under these statutes. The general practice is as follows:

Someone with an interest in tax delinquent property (an owner, or real estate speculator or developer) will retain a lawyer to institute foreclosure proceedings in the name of the State of Illinois. The first step is the completion of an information sheet provided by the Board of County Commissioners. The information sheet includes a description of the property, a list of unpaid taxes and penalties, and the minimum tax foreclosure bid. In practice there is generally only one bidder, the interested party, who has set the proceedings in motion through his lawyer. Both the preparation of the information sheet and consideration of the bids are checked and passed upon by the Board of County Commissioners. (Since it is the county that is in possession of the tax lien, the Board is theoretically the prime mover in the proceedings, and the State's Attorney's Office acts as legal arm of the county in bringing about the foreclosure.) The bid must state a price that includes a percentage of all unpaid taxes and penalties prior to 1947 [10] and the full value of all such claims since. The bids, however, are subject to compromise with the Board. Once the information sheet has been approved, a complaint is filed in the Clerk's Office of the Circuit or Superior Court of Cook County, the defendants being served either personally or, in most cases, by publication, since most defendants probably cannot be located. The court holds a hearing and then enters a decree (also prepared by the lawyer) ordering the property to be sold at public sale at a certain date. The successful purchaser at the sale receives a certificate of purchase from the county clerk which is subject to a two-year period of redemption.

It is not uncommon for real estate speculators to make periodic searches for property with delinquent taxes, which can be determined from the records of the County Clerk's Office. Having bought out the interests of those owners that could be located, the speculators have the property "cleared" through the foreclosure proceedings and then sell the land at a handsome profit to developers or promoters.

Tax foreclosure specialists generally work for other lawyers who represent either individual property owners or large promoters, developers, and speculators in the real estate or tax foreclosure business.

The distinguishing feature of the tax foreclosure lawyer, the advantage he has over other lawyers, and what gives him value in the eyes of the speculator or promoter or a referring lawyer is his ability to expedite these proceedings and get a low bid for his client. According to one lawyer, it is necessary to "push" complaints so that they don't "sit" in the various offices through which they must pass. He will also generally prepare the decree in advance because "you lose time if you wait until the return date to do so." With maximum pushing, according to this lawyer, the foreclosure proceedings take about four months; without pushing they could take a year. It was made quite clear by this lawyer and others that the "pushing" skill and the ability to get a low bid depend on having the proper contacts. In fact, most of the lawyers who said they used to handle such matters gave this as one of the reasons for not doing so any more:

I used to, but I never like politics—it's a filthy business. You had to know someone in the State's Attorney's Office. I did, because I knew a fellow close to ——— [a previous State's Attorney]. . . . I turn 'em over now to ———, a tax fixer. You have to give money to the State's Attorneys. He [the tax fixer] does it for lawyers—those who wouldn't do it themselves, but turn the other way when someone else does it. (40)

One tax foreclosure specialist claimed that he was able to clean up titles faster than most other lawyers. He attributed his effectiveness to knowing the right people in the State's Attorney's Office. "You have to know 'em," he said, "or you stand there for years, months." Asked if he had to do favors for them, he replied: "You do a little, not money, but go out to lunch, things like that." The other lawyer with a large volume of tax foreclosure work pointed out that you had to do favors for the clerks in the State's Attorney's Office, and the Chicago Title and Trust Company, but he wouldn't specify further what these favors were. One lawyer, a part-time employee of a very active tax foreclosure firm, was quite candid about the pay-offs. Speaking of the court clerks, he said:

For the firm I hand out five and ten dollars. I put it in the black book for the [firm's] bookkeeper. (35)

The county officials, he said, were generally "taken care of" by the client; the firm, however, has important political contacts:

If we need something from a politician, we have liaison men—on the payroll. If you want to meet ——— [a county official], well, he's a friend of So-and-so. I wouldn't handle that. I talk too much. . . . We get a tip-off the minute they file a case—we get a copy of the foreclosure. . . . The judges are not corrupt, but they know us—and they may get a Christmas present. We get certain priority, in suits called and filed. The others can sit for months. (36)

Several lawyers commented that tax foreclosure work is handled on a large scale by only a small number of lawyers (probably no more than 20), and, according to one, "if you're not a part of the ring you don't get it." (24) Another said that he got fewer and fewer such cases because, as he put it, "the real estate men and individual clients go to people who go after it actively." (8) Those who do specialize in this work will often have a staff of people working for them, helping in the large amount of detail work involved in the preparation of these proceedings. One lawyer said that this was the reason he farmed out most of his tax foreclosure work to specialists (this and because of their better connections):

They have an organization to skip-trace, to find the owner. . . . They "know the boys" and the procedures and techniques. (15)

Tax foreclosure work is considered a highly specialized, technical, detailed job, and many deliberately shy away from it for this reason. The technical aspects, however, although very time consuming and requiring close attention to detail and a great deal of checking and rechecking, do not appear to demand a high degree of technical-legal competence and probably can be learned in a relatively short period of time; it seems to be essentially a high-grade clerical or bookkeeping job. According to one young lawyer who handles a certain amount of tax foreclosure work for an older man in his suite:

It's not law but a business. A lot of nonlawyers are in it, and there's no special legal skill involved. (1)

Next in importance in the tax area are the personal property and real estate tax matters. In both areas, lawyers come in contact with the same agencies—the County Assessor's Office and the Board of Tax Appeals.[11] There are, however, differences in procedures. In personal property tax cases a schedule is presented to the County Assessor's Office giving a list of the property and its value. This schedule will either be approved, and the tax bill made out on that basis, or amended. In the latter case some adjustment will be sought with the Assessor's Office or with the county Board of Tax Appeals. In many instances the lawyer advises his client not to file a schedule, but to wait to be sued by the State, at which time a compromise can be reached. At present the State's Attorney's Office, which prosecutes these matters, will agree to a 60 per cent settlement of the amount sued for, based on the valuation by the assessor; but where a schedule is actually filed, 100 per cent must be paid. In real estate tax matters, the lawyer is attempting to obtain a reduction in the assessed value of the property from the Board of Tax Appeals or the Assessor's Office. In such cases, the lawyer may either seek a compromise with the assessor before the valuation is made public, or, after it is made public, he may still arrive at some adjustment in a hearing before the Board of Tax Appeals. The lawyer also may take objection to the tax rate. Here the tax is paid under protest and a rate objection is filed in the County Court seeking a refund. There appears, then, to be a great deal of discretion placed in the assessor and the Board in the valuation of property and in arriving at compromise settlements. Under these conditions, and where the property tax statutes are considered unrealistic, and, in the case of the personal property tax, unenforceable, the opportunity for fixing and pay-offs must be rife. Recent scandals in the Assessor's Office in connection with a federal grand jury investigation have brought to light what most people connected with these matters have always known, namely, that many lawyers give substantial consideration to the clerks and officials of these offices, whether in the form of Christmas presents, campaign contributions, or outright pay-offs, and that the lawyers who pay the most, and most regularly, generally get the best treatment.[12]

A respondent commenting on the personal property tax field indicated the significance of the wide discretion given to those administering the tax:

> The personal property tax is administered in such a way that the ordinary fellow doesn't file a return and he's rarely sued. If you're sued, you go over to the State's Attorney's Office and you make it O.K. If they really administered the law, what do you think the bill would be for International Harvester—it would be prohibitive—their inventory alone. It's principally done by negotiation, with a lot of people over in the State's Attorney's Office. There's lots of discretion in the State's Attorney's Office. If you have any influence, you establish a pattern; with a little interpretation you get by with less than what's actually charged. . . . They're always trying to revise the act—they want a realistic statute—but never with any luck. (31)

A lawyer who has more or less left the practice of law indicated the importance of doing favors for Assistant State's Attorneys in handling personal property tax matters—at least during the time when he was more active:

The State's Attorneys expected you to take care of them (lunch, send a gift). Mostly so in the personal property tax area. This was years ago. ──── used to try those cases. I wouldn't give him anything. Now he's on the bench. . . . The people without influence pay the load. The people with political influence are taken care of beforehand. There's a horrible personal property tax situation. (40)

Although the ultimate client is generally a corporation or a real estate man, the few lawyers specializing in property tax matters get most of their work from other lawyers:

I do a lot of [real estate] tax work. I file rate objections on 2,000 parcels, for example, but I can't possibly contact 2,000 people. I may know 500, but the rest comes in blocks from other lawyers—generally lawyer-real estate men. I work closely with them on almost a daily basis. If there are any questions of fact, I call them, and they participate in fees on a one-third basis. . . . There is a permanent group of about twenty-five lawyers, mostly individual practitioners or in small firms, whom I regard as individual practitioners. (6)

The referring lawyer, on his part, is usually more than happy to let someone else take care of such matters:

It [handling real estate tax objections] takes very little skill—it's connections. . . . The lawyers who do that are in small firms, about a dozen of them. They specialize in that, they may file on a thousand parcels. I may have any one year 60 to 70, to adjust amounts, issue checks. I don't have the time. (85)

It appears, then, that what for an individual lawyer may be a bothersome small item arising as an incident to his real estate or corporate-business practice, can, if handled on a volume basis, become a rather lucrative specialty. As in the tax foreclosure field, a certain degree of technical, detailed work is involved, but in both cases the work becomes highly formalized, and routinized, and generally reduced to bookkeeping operations. Again, the real skill is in the manipulation of local officials, and more time is spent negotiating with clerks and officials than in the preparation of documents, and very little time, if any, in looking up the law. One specialist said he spent (in an average week) a day and a half on the preparation of documents, and a few hours at home or on his way home reading the *Illinois State Bar Journal* or advance sheets, but fifteen to twenty hours negotiating in clerks' offices and with local officials.

Those who handle only an occasional tax matter, with a few exceptions, handle only federal income tax returns during the tax season for individuals or small business partnerships. These are generally routine, uncomplicated returns. As one lawyer pointed out:

> We [he and his sister, who is a real estate broker and insurance agent] do quite a bit of income tax work from January to April—the simpler stuff (complicated stuff I won't touch—corporate returns, for example), simpler wage stuff and small business returns. (19)

Some neighborhood practitioners have managed to build up a fairly sizable income tax practice operating on a large-volume basis during the tax season. One young lawyer who has an office in his home has been giving serious thought to going in with an older lawyer with just such a tax practice:

> There's this older lawyer . . . he has a large income tax work. He's a sick man and he's by himself. He's been there 25 or 30 years. He has a real estate broker with him, and he's really built up a large following. The income tax he has is all mine. I go down afternoons and evenings sometimes, and we're coming to terms. I may stay more permanently, working on a 50–50 basis. If I could get a part-time job in the mornings, I would work with him in the afternoons and evenings. (53)

Most of what little practice he has comes from income tax work he now gets through this older lawyer.

Another respondent who maintains an office at home works for a mortgage house and has built up a large private practice, 30 per cent of which is in income tax.

> I have a heavy income tax practice—too much. I'll have to sort it out this year. In the beginning you can't be too selective. During tax time I have 4 girls working for me, but generally work to two-three in the morning, seven days a week—generally from 6:30 to 1:00, from December 1 to April 15.

PERSONAL INJURY

The basic routine in handling a personal injury case for an injured party involves the following steps:

Building Up a File. The first document to go into the file is usually a retainer contract signed by the client. In this the client agrees to retain the attorney to institute or adjust his claim and to recover damages, giving the lawyer exclusive right to take all necessary steps to enforce his claim. The client further agrees not to settle the claim without the consent of the lawyer. In consideration of these services the client agrees that the lawyer shall retain a certain percentage of any judgment or settlement, generally one third in Chicago.

In the first interview with the client the lawyer will get the client's version of the circumstances leading up to the accident and the extent of his injuries. Later this statement and statements from the defendant and witnesses will be taken down and recorded in the form of a deposition, with attorneys for both sides present. The depositions constitute the second major item in the file. The third consists of "specials" referring to medical bills, property damage bills, statement of lost wages, and other claims for special as opposed to general damages. The final item is the medical report.

Negotiation. In practically all personal injury cases where a lawyer enters the picture representing a claimant, the defendant is insured and the negotiations take place between the claimant's lawyer and a claims adjuster (and occasionally the claims supervisor) of an insurance company.

The first step in the negotiation process is for the lawyer to notify the insurance company that his client has a claim against one of their insured. Notice will be given by a letter, a phone call, or sometimes a personal visit to the adjuster. In some instances suit will be immediately filed in court, in which case the insurance company will receive notice of a claim from the defendant. Where the lawyer has a number of claims against the same company he may wait and bring them all to the attention of the adjuster at the same time in the hope possibly of a package deal.

Most negotiations take place over the telephone, and sometimes lawyers will be on a first-name basis with adjusters they have never seen. Quite often, however, the lawyer will go to the offices of the insurance company: "The phone is more convenient, but if you go over and talk to them it's a lot better." Only two lawyers said that they preferred to have the adjuster come to their office.

After the adjuster has been notified of the claim he will usually ask for a copy of the "specials," and the lawyer, in an effort to reach a settlement, will generally comply.

> They want to know the doctor's report, the bills, time lost, and so on. I supply that—you have to—otherwise they won't co-operate. (32)

> They'll say, "Mail me the specials." Formerly I refused to mail them. Before, I'd read 'em off to negotiate a settlement, discuss injury and liability, and try to reach a figure; but you still wouldn't get to a meeting of the minds, you'd still need conferences. So to save time I give them the specials, mail 'em in, and then they call you. (33)

> If they ask for the doctor's bill, or if their doctor can see your client—I often volunteer it—or they may ask how often the client was off from work, I tell them; you find out that that attitude sets well with these people. (36)

The fact that it now takes four to five years in Chicago to get a personal injury case to trial gives a bargaining edge to the insurance companies, since they are obviously in a better position to wait it out.[13] The lawyer, even though he may have built up a large volume of cases, which ensures a more or less regular flow of recoveries, still has to deal with the impatience of individual clients. Under these conditions he is under some pressure to reach an early settlement, particularly on the smaller claims; and the insurance companies naturally prefer to clear up as many claims as possible. Thus it would appear that the majority of the smaller claims are probably disposed of rather quickly.[14] With the bigger claims, however, the insurance companies will hold out longer and in these cases the greater resources of the more successful personal injury lawyers may often make the difference in the size of the eventual recovery. As one lawyer put it:

> If you have any kind of a case they don't give you anything at the beginning—you have to keep your client in line. They hate to wait, but if you can wait it out you get a better settlement at trial. (33)

In order to keep his client in line and also as an inducement to get the client in the first place, the lawyer often finds it necessary to advance not only the costs of litigation, if suit is instituted, but living expenses as well.

Contact with the Courts.　Some lawyers, as we have said, will immediately institute suit as a matter of course, presumably in the belief that this will bolster their bargaining position with the insurance companies. Most of them, however, will try to settle first, and only if they are unsuccessful will file suit.[15]

Final Settlement or Judgment.　The check in payment of the settlement or judgment is generally made out by the insurance company to both the lawyer and the client. The lawyer will have the check endorsed by the client, and after he has taken out his fee, whatever advances he has made, and made sure the doctor has been paid, will remit to the client a check for the balance.

The personal injury practice of half the specialists in

this area—the lower-level practitioners—is restricted to building up a file and to efforts at negotiation with claims adjusters. The paper work is routine and relatively uncomplicated. Contact with the courts is generally limited to filing complaints or motions and an occasional appearance; only one such lawyer mentioned that he ever tried a case. The bigger cases are referred out to other lawyers if they cannot be readily settled.

One lower-level personal injury lawyer gave me the following account of his practice. Most of his day is spent in the office—little or no time in other lawyers' offices or in the courts. He turns over his trial work to a particular lawyer:

> He has one now. Sometimes you get a whole splurge, and then none. He may have started three or four this year.

Contact with the insurance companies is principally over the telephone:

> At one time they were all in the Insurance Exchange Building. Now they all have branches. I can't go out to Park Ridge, so negotiation is mostly over the phone.

He reads nothing in the way of legal material and engages in no research. His paper work is reduced to a rather simple routine:

> Preparation work, for adjustment—doctors' reports, and so on. I have three classes of matters: files pending, files being prepared, and suit files—and then I have my files in the cabinets. I take a slip of paper, mark down what I need on the slip of white paper. [Looking through some files on his desk] This one is not ready yet; this one is.

Reflecting on the description of his work he had just given me, he added:

> Pete [his employer when he first started out in practice] used to say, the busiest lawyer works two hours a day. That list I gave you, that could be crushed into an hour and a half.

He gave the following description of what he had done on the day previous to the interview:

> Yesterday from 2:00 to 4:00 I listened to the World Series. In the morning I checked on a case in trial, a case about four years old [which he had referred to another lawyer], personal injury and property damage—three cars involved, ours is the innocent car. I called a party with reference to a matter still pending; a woman was injured, in the hospital, I want to find out when I can interview her. I called a client and asked her to send me a certain letter required for settlement of a claim. Checked by phone another party involved with a client of mine in an accident —trying to locate. Checked through files, to see what I needed from clients. I discussed with ——— [another lawyer in the suite] a probate matter I had referred to him. I also discussed with ——— [same lawyer] a suit—I turned over to him a big suit in behalf of a minor, rescission in purchase of an auto. I mailed out certified copies of documents to an insurance company in an effort toward settling a matter. And stuff I'd rather not tell you. (88)

Another lower-level practitioner provided a similar picture of this type of practice. He is rarely in court except to file a complaint in the clerk's office. On the days he is downtown he spends about an hour talking to adjusters in insurance company offices. A good part of his day is apparently spent in his office, but doing what was not clear.

> *Interviewer:* Do you spend any time reading legal material?
> *Respondent:* I'm ashamed to tell you, not even an hour a week. You can say I get by on cursory knowledge of the law. But it's mostly the same thing, not just bluffing.
> *Interviewer:* Do you spend any time preparing legal documents?
> *Respondent:* Zero. Well, pleadings, yes, but most are in subrogation cases, and I use a form, filling in the date, and so on, so it doesn't take too much time. If it's in the Circuit or Superior Court it's just a simple two-page document.

How much time does he spend negotiating?

> I write a letter on a thing, call on the phone; sometimes I settle it right away. If you wait for the insurance company to respond to the letter, however, it may take six months. If it's an out-of-town company, I'll send a letter. The busy people in this business have forms for letters. I try to keep down the stenographic work. I try to clean it up on the phone, if I can. If I know them, and it's a case that should be settled, I call 'em on the phone. Insurance companies do that too.

He generally spends some time with clients, most often in the early evening:

> They work during the day, and I don't like to see them lose a day's work. Sometimes as often as three or four nights a week—I combine it with other work. I make some calls in the evening—it's a little more relaxed.

"If you don't go to court," he concluded, "almost any lawyer can handle a personal injury case—attorney's lien, and negotiations for settlement—it's not complicated."

He gave the following account of his work on the day before the interview:

> Yesterday was a hard day, I was trying to catch up [he had been away on vacation]. I got down at 9:30, had breakfast, went to the john—oh, don't put that in—read the mail. Yesterday I bought some tickets at the Orchestral Association, and I picked them up. I looked up a man in the Gas Building who owes me some money—he wasn't in. I got some shirts at Marshall Field's; picked up some medicine for my mother. I just couldn't get started yesterday. I opened a file with some checks I collected at my insurance company office [they send him most of his subrogation work]. I saw another client, an insurance agent. I do his general work, I collect accounts for him. He told me I lost a beautiful personal injury case while I was away— a little boy was injured. I told him a lawyer needs a vacation—but that made me feel bad to lose it. He could have had sense enough to call someone else in the office here. I made some phone calls. Another lawyer called me about a trip west he was contemplating—I spoke to him for half an hour. I had dinner at five, stayed down till nine, typed up some letters [in connection with subrogation claims], and I called up one or two people involved in a case. (44)

One of the distinguishing features of the upper-level personal injury practitioners is their greater effectiveness in negotiating with the insurance companies. This results partly from the fact that they handle a larger volume of cases and are in a better position to establish a more permanent relationship with the adjusters, but also because they have made it quite clear that if pressed they will be able and in a position to take a case to trial. One upper-level lawyer pointed out:

> Over the years if you deal with the same men, they know you're willing to fight and litigate, if necessary. You develop rapport. They are the most important people in any practice. They may settle with you where they won't with others, because of the regard they have for you, the fact that you treat them well, give them information. . . . When the adjuster has limited authority, you see the supervisor. It gets to a point where you call each other by first names. They will tell me things in their file so I can reevaluate things in my file. They don't do that with strangers. (36)

Another upper-level lawyer gave a similar, although somewhat more aggressive, appraisal of his effectiveness:

> I've had successful results in settlements. The insurance companies know that I will fight them down the line—four, five years if necessary. In cases where clients are offered only $500 I've got $6,500, $7,000. They may have had dealings with shysters and chasers, but when they find out that ——— [respondent's name] gets $6,500 in a case they didn't think was worth that much—well . . . I take cases worthwhile fighting through to the end. (33)

The greater effectiveness of upper-level lawyers rests also on their ability to wait out a good case, and that usually entails advancing living expenses and other costs to the client:

> They're not advances, but loans to clients. Many can't work, are hospitalized, and you have to help them.

> *Interviewer:* That requires capital, I suppose.
>
> *Respondent:* Yes, you should have a large working capital. That $30,000 suit against the railroad, he was offered $5,000—he had no money and they knew of his impecuniousness. So you have to lend them money. (22)

> I occasionally advance funds. It depends. They call on us to do that less than in years gone by. Many carry accident and hospital insurance. If they're disabled and need financial insurance, we pay, as a loan so they can feed their family. I won't support a client indefinitely, only six or eight weeks—he must have a financial interest. If he's supported, he forgets how much his case is worth, and when we finally pay him, the net cash payment is less than he expected. I'll always compete, though. Those that require complete financing are the railroad cases—I get them only occasionally. If I got them I'd be very happy to finance 'em—he'll still have a substantial sum to collect after the advances. (36)

Upper-level personal injury lawyers reported spending over three times as much time in trial work as do the lower-level lawyers. The former are not only more active in trial work, but it would appear that they put in over twice as much time in the library and in reading legal material, and considerably more time with clients and preparing briefs and legal documents than do their lower-level colleagues.

The clients of both lower- and upper-level personal injury lawyers are generally working-class individuals. Where the two groups of lawyers differ is in the size of the claim brought by their clients and in how they obtain their clients.

Lower-level lawyers handle the smaller claims and only rarely get a big case. Not one received 10 per cent or more of his business on referrals from other lawyers; most said they relied heavily on recommendations from other clients, friends, and acquaintances. A lower-level respondent who relies on recommendations pointed out the necessity for giving gratuities to people who bring in business:

> If they send in business on a regular basis, I give a gratuity; if it's an occasional referral, I don't have to. I give gratuities in about 10 to 15 per cent of the cases.
> *Interviewer:* Have you ever been approached by chasers?
> *Respondent:* One chaser approached me. He had leads to business—he was working with the police. He wanted $40 a head, in advance, and a percentage of the fee. I didn't like the cases he had, and I was a little leery of starting up with that. He'd sign up clients on the street. I didn't approve of it. (32)

An insurance broker friend sends him some personal injury matters, in return for which the broker generally gets a percentage of the fee, "same as a lawyer."

Another lower-level lawyer said that he gets a few cases from doctors and occasionally something from garagemen. Asked if he gave gratuities to those who send him business, he replied:

> Oh, yes, a reward for appreciation. I bought a lighter and cigarettes, but they don't come with their hands out. If I give, it's voluntary on my part. (88)

Another lawyer denied giving gratuities, but added:

> I get most of my clients on referrals from other clients. So, when I wind up a case for a client, I invite the client for drinks or lunch—it leaves a good going-away impression. (48)

Upper-level lawyers not only attract bigger cases but have more stable, permanent sources of business. Most of these practitioners rely heavily on referrals from other lawyers, several reporting that well over half their business is obtained in this manner. The referring lawyers are rewarded—usually willingly—with a third to a half of the fee. One lawyer who generally pays out half his fee to the referring attorney noted:

> You pay more than that to chasers—you also have to reimburse the cops. Chasers get one third to 40 per cent just as an investigator's fee. You keep these people on your payroll. But it's your case—like buying a bond. (27)

All upper-level practitioners said that they got at least some cases from doctors and some said that doctors supplied up to a third of their practice. The usual arrangement with the doctor, I was informed, is: "No pay, just protection. When a case is settled, we see that their bills are paid." The lawyer ensures that the doctor will be paid by having the client sign an authorization permitting the lawyer to deduct the doctor's fee from the total settlement. As one lawyer explained:

> I made sure he [the doctor] had a decent medical fee—made sure it was protected. He wanted to get an authorization that he would get paid, a direction from the client, an informal agreement. I give the money, the check, to the patient and he endorses it over to the doctor.

Some lawyers take more direct responsibility for payment:

> I pay for his [the doctor's] services; he doesn't look to the client. I pay whether we win or lose. (45)

Previous clients, garage mechanics, policemen, hospital attendants, and for some, the professional chaser may become important sources of business for the upper-level practitioner. With these people the lawyer generally pays a flat fee, or gratuity, for each case sent in. A lawyer who receives well over half his personal injury cases on recommendations from previous clients and others explained:

> If a colored guy sends me a case, a $200 case, I give him $10. If you don't, he won't remember you the next time. There isn't a lawyer in Chicago who doesn't do it—some kind of gratuity to people who bring in business.
> *Interviewer:* Do you have regular ones?
> *Respondent:* Yes, insurance brokers, doctors—your study will be hard on individual practitioners. The guys in the Bar Association, the big defense firms, and insurance companies make it difficult to bring cases, they put into the Canons that you can't give a present. I'm against organized chasing; it doesn't let a guy like me get cases. I don't have any professional chasers. I'm too frightened to use them. Mine come from referrals. With certain ones I don't give a gratuity. I don't give anything to my brothers, and a great percentage of business came and was developed through my brothers. I get referrals from foremen, and they don't get anything. My brother has an associate doctor, and they get nothing except free legal advice. And I don't give friends money. For 20 per cent I have to give gratuities. With colored you have to give them something, and they're very appreciative—and they're good for getting business. Fifteen per cent of my clients are colored. They're warm, goodhearted people, and if they trust a lawyer they trust him down the line. (28)

Later when I came back to finish my interview with this lawyer he was somewhat apprehensive about his discussion of gratuities and said he wanted to make it quite clear that he gave a gratuity only infrequently:

> I don't enjoy giving it, it comes out of my pocket. In most situations, 85 to 90 per cent of the cases are referred to me by clients and with no gratuity except a thank you. I intend to sell people that I'm a good lawyer, concerned with their welfare. . . . The great bulk are nongratuity, and I'm thankful for that. (28)

Another lawyer said that a large part of his personal injury practice came from "people in a position to get cases —if people are in an accident, they find out." When asked if he paid them anything, he replied:

> I send them far less than a chaser gets—mainly to compensate for their time. It's never over 20 per cent of a fee— and it's payable after I get the fee. I get 10 to 15 per cent of the cases that way. (27)

Another upper-level lawyer, when asked if he gave gratuities to people who sent him cases, said:

> I might send a gift. Most of the time, however, I can accommodate by legal service you don't charge for—wage garnishment suits by tradesmen, domestic problems, and so on.
> *Interviewer:* Have you dealt with policemen?
> *Respondent:* A few policemen have approached me, but they didn't seek me out; they came in the office in connection with an investigation and asked if I would handle stuff. I didn't.
> *Interviewer:* Have you used chasers?
> *Respondent:* That type of business—first, something about it is abhorrent. These chasers put you under pres-

sure—they run the lawyer, the lawyer doesn't run them. You become dependent on them, and if you depend on them it could hurt you if they turn from you. They'll keep you busy if you do a volume of business. And their demands are exorbitant. Some want 40 per cent, some 50 per cent—the good chaser wants more than a third. I never get business from policemen. I'd have no objection if I could tell the client they were referred by a policeman, but they won't let you. (36)

This lawyer's familiarity with the difficulties and dangers of doing business with chasers may very well be based on experience. He indicated that until quite recently he employed a full-time investigator, often a euphemism for chaser, who was responsible for a large share of his overhead costs. He claimed that the investigator charged on the basis of "time put in, not a percentage. The one I used was a lawyer. They adjust their charges accordingly; if they have good information they charge—after the work is done." Asked if they also brought in business, he replied, "No. But occasionally they do." Although the respondent made no mention of it, there would seem to be some relationship between the assertion "I'm not doing as much business recently" and the fact that he no longer employed an investigator.

A flat denial of using chasers or runners came from another upper-level practitioner:

I have no runners or lead men.
Interviewer: How do you get your business?
Respondent: I represent used car dealers. I do favors for them—review a contract and so on. In return they send me clients. I sit here and they come to me. I also get some from insurance companies.

Interviewer: What do you do for them?

Respondent: I'm friendly. I take 'em out for dinner.

Interviewer: Do you know about chasers, aren't there supposed to be some who use a walkie-talkie system in patrolling hospitals?

Respondent: Yah, around Cook County and South-town. I know the lawyers who use that. Sure it hurts me; I might get some of it otherwise.

Interviewer: Do you pay for leads?

Respondent: No, I give them service. (22)

Most of his cases, he said, come from "happy, satisfied customers." However, considering his income (he had just received a check for $30,000 in settlement of a claim against a railroad), and his flat denial of any competition in the personal injury field (most complained that it was highly competitive), it would seem very unlikely that he does not use some means other than giving service to induce people to send him cases.

Another lawyer relying principally on recommendations gave the following explanation for not having to "buy" cases:

I never gave a gratuity in all my years of practice. I could have had ten lawyers working for me. There have been opportunities, but I never split a fee or give a gratuity —except going out for lunch. . . . I don't do a volume personal injury business; I take cases that are worth fighting through to the end. I don't take bad cases, you compromise on a volume basis, I don't have chasers giving me a volume of business—that requires too large an overhead. . . . Cases come to me on my terms, on the confidence they have in me, and on the belief that I would get the best deal down the line. If I had a chaser, then I would have to meet competition. Mine is reference work, clients or friends. If it were volume work, I'd be settling 200 cases, and not 15. (33)

He did mention, however, that he hires someone to do a certain amount of "investigative work."

The problem of getting business in the personal injury field is undoubtedly aggravated by the existence of a few very successful personal injury lawyers who rely almost exclusively on highly organized methods of solicitation, co-operating with chasers and others who have made it their business to locate the potentially most rewarding cases. These people, armed with retainer contracts in blank, have developed quite elaborate and seemingly efficient procedures that enable them to be first in time to reach potentially lucrative clients. They have contacts with police, particularly in accident squads, and contacts in hospitals with interns, doctors, nurses, and ambulance drivers. It is well known, for example, that certain hospitals are "controlled" by certain chasers. As one lawyer put it:

———— [a well-known personal injury lawyer] makes a million a year from ———— Hospital. If I went in there, the police would escort me out. An outsider can't get in— I'd be picked up for unethical practice. (28)

The best-organized chasers have automobiles patrolling hospitals with two-way radios and can be informed almost instantly of the admission of an accident case. A chaser, often working with one of the doctors or interns, will be at the patient's bedside with a contract ready to "sign him up" as soon as the patient has recovered sufficiently to write his name. The lawyer quoted above reported just such an incident:

At 2:15 a court reporter came over, and we went out to a client's home to take a statement. He was badly hurt and had been taken to a hospital, and when he regained consciousness the doctor assigned to him—gee, I hope this will be confidential—introduced a young man to him saying, "He'll be your lawyer, sign here." In addition, they took his savings account book. I've got a sworn statement from the court reporter. The patient wanted to hire me. He had been referred to me by his employer. (28)

Although proportionately few lawyers get business in this way, such practices have the effect of taking a large number of the most lucrative personal injury cases out of the market. Most lower-level lawyers complained rather bitterly of this situation:

Oh, yes, [the competition] in the personal injury field is very severe. I get the leftovers, either those I get to first or people who are conscious and don't fall prey. (32)

In my work my only competition is from ambulance chasers. (44)

Oh, yes, there's much competition from other lawyers in the field of personal injury, for one. There are so many specialists in that field and ambulance chasers; it's increasingly difficult to get business in that field. The only business I get is through the medium of referrals from clients and friends. (48)

There definitely is [competition] in the personal injury field, particularly. [It's] the only serious place where there is competition.
Interviewer: Has it hurt you?
Respondent: Do you mean in reference to ambulance chasing? It hurts every lawyer who doesn't participate in it.
Interviewer: Have you been directly hurt?

Respondent: Just once. My uncle was injured and he was immediately signed up by a policeman—or an ambulance driver. I was disgusted with my uncle. He got a small settlement. (17)

Yes [there is competition]. Personal injury, for one. I've had chasers take two or three cases from me. (2)

There were complaints of price cutting as well as chasing:

There is a problem [of competition]; sometimes it's very severe. I have a case here. Well, this lady, she tells me a lawyer will handle the case for 20 per cent. That's asinine, nobody can do that. The usual rate is one third and sometimes one half. There's a lot of competition from unethical, unscrupulous lawyers. I would do better if they were done away with, my practice would improve. (88)

Only one lower-level lawyer denied that there was a problem of competition, and he was the only one with a regular source of business. Ten insurance broker friends provided him with one half of his personal injury business.

One or two upper-level lawyers complained of competition as bitterly as their lower-level colleagues:

A lawyer like myself rarely gets a good case—only by accident. The police are our biggest competitors, and the big ambulance chasers—two of them sit as chairmen on committees of the ——— Bar Association. (28)

I feel the competition today is from the young lawyers. They'll do business with chasers [because they think that is] the only way of getting business.
Interviewer: But doesn't that take a lot of money?
Respondent: Yes, but their fathers-in-law will bankroll them. . . . In so far as there are chasers and lawyers buy-

ing from chasers, it cuts down on the volume of my business. If a doctor I know had first crack I might get it, but if he doesn't, I can't. (36)

Most upper-level lawyers, however, either felt that there was no competition or if there was they didn't feel that it particularly hurt them.

Three of the lawyers I interviewed are presently employed as claim supervisors by insurance companies; two had particularly strong views on the personal injury practitioner. We shall close this section with their comments:

A large percentage of the legal representation of personal injury clients in Chicago is got by unethical means. The national average is 25 per cent representation by counsel; in Chicago 75 per cent are represented by counsel. If the police are called to the scene of an accident, there is no foreseeable chance but that active and vigorous solicitation will follow. Corrupt politicians are on the payrolls of chasers, doctors are on their payrolls and turn in fake medical reports or [reports that] are grossly overemphasized or misinterpreted, and sometimes fraudulent. Lawyers rig up cases, expand, magnify and distort. Many are a disgrace to the profession, but I have to show I consider them brilliant—you get quite cynical. I haven't seen a true medical bill in I don't know how long. We don't even use them as an estimate. The lawyer wants it the higher the better—and that induces the doctor to bill high. I can name hot spots over the country, from the defense point of view, where judges are openly corrupt. Not so here, although the judges fall far short of what one expects in law schools—they lack ability. . . . There are too many unqualified men in the profession in Chicago, incapable of doing a job; they are mostly night law school graduates and very inadequately trained. (72)

I don't think much of the aspect of the law I'm in here, personal injury, the so-called negligence field. It's a sad part of the general law field. If you saw how cases are settled and built up with that portion of the profession in the personal injury field, in metropolitan areas like Chicago—it's really rank. Makes you feel a little less proud of the profession, or of that part of the profession you come in contact with. A real shame. (59)

DIVORCE

Some idea of the nature of divorce work may be gained from the following workday account of an upper-level specialist in this area:

> I get down around 9:30. My work is prepared the night before and is on my desk—the files I'm going to work on. I glance at the mail, see if there are any petitions in it that might require an appearance in court. In divorce you get only a certain number of hours of notice. If a lad is served with notice to come in tomorrow, I'll call the lawyer on the phone and tell him, ask him to put it over till I know I'm in. [That is, until he is certain that he wants to represent the client. He was speaking of a case that had just been referred to him by another lawyer and he had not yet had a chance to speak with the client. During the interview he called the other lawyer in the case and explained to him that he would have to see the client first, discuss fees, and so on, before he knew if he would be "in," and therefore asked the other lawyer to "kick it over" to Tuesday. He was holding the phone so I could hear the other lawyer say that it would be all right but that if another lawyer

came in there'd be another continuance and that would put him in a difficult position. The respondent was a little exasperated and told the other attorney he just couldn't say if he would be in before he saw the client. The other lawyer finally acquiesced, the respondent mugging throughout. When he hung up, he said that if it were the other way around, there would have been no question about it.] In general I'm in court two or three cases a day. I have 50 active cases, and in the course of a day I may work on 15 or 20, and handle two on motion. I was in [court] on three yesterday. That's the morning.

In the afternoon I have conference work with clients, and lawyers. A woman came in to see me one day last week with a petition in her hand, a notice to appear in a Champaign court. She comes in with this story: Last year her husband got a divorce in Champaign. There were two minor children, and the agreement was to let him have custody for one year. Now he wants permanent custody. She heard about me through someone and she wants to retain me. I told her she would do better to get someone in Champaign. I called ——— [a lawyer in Champaign] and asked him if he would take it, and he said he would. He wanted me to be in the picture and she felt she wanted me to join in. Well, I asked him to contact the other [the husband's] lawyer. He [the other lawyer] was adamant about having it [the hearing] on Monday. I wanted time. I wanted it heard after Labor Day; we wanted a continuance. Well, we found out that we had a continuance till October 7, but I'm mad because I know his [the husband's lawyer's] strategy: he'll be in Oklahoma then [the husband, an army officer, was being transferred there, and that was the reason he wanted permanent custody]. Now I want an injunction to restrain him from leaving or to turn over the kids to her and then leave. So there were a few more telephone calls. Now I'm having difficulty reaching my client—I need her signature on a petition.

I put through a divorce a couple of weeks ago—the fellow took the divorce. Now there is a petition to set aside, the woman was incensed—*she* wants to take the divorce. (38)

Like several other lawyers handling divorce matters, as we shall see, this lawyer places particular emphasis on the marriage counseling aspect of his practice and prides himself on his skill in bringing about reconciliations.

I go further with my clients—I do something the top guy doesn't. There is a case in this town, for example, but I wouldn't take it unless I could bring them together. I know the people too well, and that's probably the reason I don't have it. Well, this fellow is an attorney. He caught his wife in an act of adultery—it's a suit in adultery and alienation of affections against her parents. He called me as a friend and I talked to him for an hour and made suggestions. I didn't charge him, I wouldn't take his case. This is not in criticism of the other lawyer, but if they took time to recognize the clients' problems, they'd get into less rigmarole across the street [the County Building]. I try to size them up that way, and try to patch them up.

If, when he sizes them up, he finds that emotional problems are the cause of the difficulty, he refers them to a psychiatrist.

I have seven going to one, an analyst, I use. I try to patch 'em up if I can. For example, a woman comes in very distressed. She asks me to help her hold on to her husband. It has to be hush, hush—a prominent husband (I am *not* in the papers, that's why she came to me).[16] This boy is sexually satisfied only when his wife picks up a stranger off the street and he can watch. He actually drills holes in the floor—these things take place in the basement. She loves this boy, he's a good boy in all other respects, a good provider, etc.—if only she can get over this hurdle. I send for the boy. He admits it and says what's wrong. I realize what it is, what they call voyeurism, the problem is to get him to see that he needs help. I told him that his wife is sick and needs help (which is partially true, she indicated it to me, she needs treatment) and I ask for his co-operation, and I say if I don't get it, it will be the end of the marriage, and it will all break wide open. I recommend a good analyst. It's hard to get an appointment with an analyst in this town. This man I can call and get an appointment for clients almost any time. We get the progress reports from him.

Interviewer: What is the fee arrangement with the psychiatrist?

Respondent: We are each paid separately by the client-patient. Some people speak to me about things they won't tell an analyst—you have to hold their hand.

Most of this respondent's time is spent either in conference—with clients or lawyers—or in the courts. He spends an average of about two hours a day in court, mostly filing suits, but also trying some cases. He stated that he had six trials last year that he carried right through but that most were settled short of trial. He spends very little time reading legal material or preparing documents:

> I have a sharp girl—I have dictation down to minutes— ten minutes to dictate a petition. It's mostly pleadings and drafting decrees. The girl handles the form work.

Most conferences with lawyers on the other side are held in his office, since he represents principally women, and the custom is to hold the conference in the office of the wife's lawyer.

The respondent stated that there are about twelve specialists in divorce law in Chicago. Asked if he considered himself to be the number two man, he smiled and said:

> According to money, well, there are a lot in it. I've only been in it for eight years, really, some of the others have been in for twenty-five to thirty years. But I feel as if I do as good or better a job for clients. (38)

Several lawyers mentioned that in addition to divorce they occasionally handle an adoption proceeding, and that incidental to their divorce work they may have to deal with alimony or nonsupport problems.

The work of the divorce lawyer brings him in contact with the courts to a greater extent than lawyers engaged in other fields of practice. In fact, most of the divorce lawyer's working day seems to be spent either in the courts, in the clerk's office, in hearings before a judge, or in consultation with clients. Contact with the client tends to be of a more intimate nature and closer to the doctor-patient relationship than is the case in other fields of individual law practice. In view of the fact that the client is forced to go further in disclosing matters of a personal nature than is true, for example, in the case of someone wanting to buy a piece of property or to incorporate a small business, the divorce lawyer may find himself cast in the role of an adviser or marriage counselor. Several lawyers described their work in this area as marriage counseling and seemed to take a certain amount of pride in their ability to ferret out emotional difficulties and bring about reconciliations.

One lawyer in describing his practice said that he did a

lot of marriage counseling, and added: "And I'm fairly successful in keeping people together." Asked how often he handled such matters, he replied:

> For a while, it was fairly often—maybe two or three times a month. It goes in spurts. There are two cases now where I'm trying to get the parties together. I try to do this especially where there are children.
>
> *Interviewer:* Do you charge a fee?
>
> *Respondent:* Well, they usually come in seeking a divorce or to defend on a divorce action. Most can't afford to pay very much—I charge them something, but I lose money on it—sometimes nothing, I do a good deed. (16)

Another lawyer with a relatively small divorce practice, in speaking of his work in this area, pointed out:

> Under divorce I do a lot of family counseling that never reaches the courts—friends of yours, you try to reconcile them. Usually one wants the divorce right away, so it's a selling job. I charge them a $25 an hour consultation fee. (33)

A collections lawyer who gets just a few divorce cases had just been successful in reconciling a couple:

> I brought 'em together, like the goofy guy I am. I saved a marriage—big me—and got $35 for it. (84)

A lawyer who is exclusively engaged in divorce work compared his practice with that of a doctor:

> The divorce practice is an emotional kind of business. (We're analogous to doctors, and I work with many psychiatrists.) They are sick, neurotic people who need help. (38)

Several lawyers stated that one of the things they en-
joyed most in their practice was to effect a reconciliation.
One, with largely a neighborhood practice, recalled:

> For example, there was a couple with two small kids, one
> a six months' old baby. I told the judge he should try to
> reconcile them. Well, he did, and they finally walked out
> hand in hand. I was thrilled—of course that was what my
> client wanted, a reconciliation. It didn't work out, unfortu-
> nately. (20)

The image that many individual divorce lawyers have
of themselves as marriage counselors is probably in part
an effort to compensate for the generally low regard in
which divorce practice is held, and partly a reflection of
the desire to be identified with higher status professionals.
Divorce lawyers, even those who have every intention of
maintaining the highest ethical standards, are frequently
forced into the position where they have to either manu-
facture evidence or elicit from their clients in court patently untrue or distorted statements in order to meet the
statutory grounds for divorce. Very often divorce proceedings, particularly in uncontested cases, are considered both
by the public and by many lawyers to be nothing more
than a fraudulent stage show.[17] Under these conditions the
divorce lawyer finds himself in the position of a kind of
divorce broker, acting in collusion with the court and the
parties seeking a divorce to bring about a desired end
which in many cases can only be realized with a certain
amount of tongue-in-cheek assistance by the court.

The self-esteem of the divorce lawyer is further threatened at the neighborhood level of divorce practice, where
he may find himself in the midst of lower-class domestic
brawls, some ending up in the police courts, others in the

divorce courts. The fact that divorce cases bring relatively large fees for what is often only a perfunctory service—and many less successful individual practitioners probably depend on a certain number of quick divorce fees to pull them through—helps to offset the disreputable features already indicated. Equally, if not more effective, however, is the upgrading of this type of practice that is apparently intended by defining it as marriage counseling.

A further feature that might be mentioned, and one that crops up in the answers to the question of what gives them their biggest kick in practice, is the sense of accomplishment, and the readily observable result in very human terms that is provided when a couple has been reconciled. There is little occasion elsewhere in the individual lawyer's practice for this kind of satisfaction.

Those respondents with a lower-level type of practice usually handle simple, uncontested divorces for a neighborhood clientele. That this type of divorce practice is often only a step removed from the local police court was clearly pointed out by one respondent:

> I was a people's lawyer. I did police court work, divorce, a real estate deal here or there, a combination of transient and permanent clients. There was divorce and separate maintenance work—quarrels between husband and wife and between neighbors. Some went to the police court, some I straightened out in the office. (20)

These lawyers only rarely get a divorce case on referral from other lawyers. Most of their business, apparently, comes in on recommendations from other clients, acquaintances, and occasionally from policemen, ministers, or bartenders.

Upper-level divorce practitioners have more middle-class clients (in cases usually involving a substantial property settlement), rely less on neighborhood sources but more on referrals from other lawyers and the notoriety and publicity that is achieved by representing "society" and celebrity clients than is true of lower-level lawyers.

As a final note let us consider the very interesting ethnic division of labor in the divorce area. Catholic lawyers are prohibited from helping clients to seek a divorce if the marriage is one that is recognized by the Catholic Church. If he is approached by such a client, it is the lawyer's duty to refer him to the office of the Chancellor of the Archdiocese, where petitions for divorce and separate maintenance are received and considered. The position of the Church is presented by the following remarks of two high-ranking officials:

> Any Catholic who wishes to approach the civil courts for either a divorce or separate maintenance must receive permission from the Bishop of the Diocese before proceeding in the civil courts. We hear these petitions and have been doing so for some fifteen years. In the beginning there was almost universal opposition on the part of all lawyers to co-operating with these laws of the Church. I am sure, however, that their opposition was based on a lack of understanding as to the laws of the Church and also as to the part they must of necessity play in co-operating with these laws. At the present time we are receiving co-operation from about 75 per cent of the Catholic lawyers and from about one third of the non-Catholic lawyers. The Catholic lawyers give this co-operation either because they are convinced of their duty to do so or because they think that we should be brought into marital difficulties. Non-Catholic lawyers would do it for the latter

reason only. Personally, I am a bit optimistic that as time goes on the co-operation of lawyers will be more and more frequent.[18]

Even if the non-Catholic is seeking a separate maintenance rather than divorce, the attorney must ascertain whether there is any hope of reconciliation. He is not justified in taking such cases merely for the fee without any investigation as to the lawfulness of his client's petition and intention.[19]

Only four of the Catholic lawyers in the sample indicated that as much as 10 per cent of their practice was in divorce, and almost all of them stated that they would not handle a divorce case involving Catholics without first "clearing" it through the Chancery Office. Two mentioned that their divorce practice had fallen off in recent years since the Church had been intensifying its efforts to have Catholic lawyers comply with its rules on divorce.

> *Interviewer:* Have you been restrained in any way by the Church in taking divorce cases?
> *Respondent:* I used not to be, but I have in the last four-five years. I'm appreciating their work. I won't handle it now unless I get the go-ahead from the Chancery Office. (34)

> Since this recent Church decision I don't do as much divorce work as I used to. I used to have a lot. Now, if Catholics are involved, I won't handle it. I'm willing to go along with them on that. (8)

One lawyer pointed out that this situation resulted in throwing most of the divorce work to the Jewish lawyers:

> Catholic lawyers, you know, are forbidden from taking divorces, and as a result most of them go to Jewish law-

yers, and it works out best that way. I can handle a non-Catholic divorce without going through the Chancery Office, but because I'm restrained from handling Catholic divorces, I just don't go after that kind of business. (42)

Although Jewish lawyers appear to have an edge on divorce practice, Negro lawyers also seem to get a sizable number of such matters—in fact, we find many more Negro specialists in this than in any other area of practice. Unlike the Jewish lawyers, their clientele is generally limited to members of their own ethnic group.

WILL-PROBATE-ESTATE

The will-probate-estate field includes drawing up and probating wills, and administering decedents' estates.

The preparation of a will, where a small estate is involved, is generally a routine matter based on one of several forms. Although some respondents may charge up to $35 or $40 for the preparation and execution of a will (reducing to writing, signing, and attesting of the will), most will generally charge much less as an accommodation or inducement for other business:

> I make a lot of wills and charge very little—as a complimentary deal; you make it for clients and their friends. (94)

When a lawyer draws up a will he assumes in most cases that he will probate it upon the testator's death, and act as either executor of the estate or attorney for the executor.

Not infrequently lawyers will keep the original of the will in their possession in order to ensure getting the much more lucrative probate and estate business, and for this reason many are more than willing to cut their fees for drawing a will. Sometimes a bank or trust company will be named as executor in the will, in which case the lawyer, if he recommended the bank or trust company, will generally be assured of handling the legal end of the probate and estate job. As one lawyer put it: "Their policy is that the lawyer who draws up the will will handle the estate if the trust company is named as trustee." (16) In these instances, or where the bank refers the client to a lawyer, it is not uncommon for the bank or trust company to prepare the will for the lawyer and sometimes even have it typed up. Thus one lawyer, no longer in private practice, recalled:

> If you're just out of law school you go to the trust company and you tell them your client wants them as executor (and that's all they want), they will draft the will for you, spend days with you, they'll even type it for you, and when you go back to the client, they act as if they never saw it before, and they'll say: "That's a good will, Mr. ———— [respondent's name], that's a particularly well-phrased paragraph." Well, that embarrasses you a little. (40)

When the bank is acting as executor in administering an estate, there is generally little for the lawyer to do but go over what has already been prepared by the bank—the inventories, accounts, and so on. The balance of skills, competence, and resources is generally tipped in favor of the local bank or trust company.

> The ordinary practitioner can't handle large matters involving large income tax matters, estate problems, trusts.

The ordinary practitioner is not equipped with skill and knowledge—he's just as happy to refer it to a trust department. He does some of the legal work, some of the paper work, and gets some of the fee. (24)

Several mentioned that they had working arrangements with local banks, the understanding being that the bank would refer clients to them on will-probate-estate matters in return for which the lawyer would send them business—such as accounts and trust. More often than not, however, respondents viewed the banks and trust companies as dangerous competitors; next to real estate brokers, banks were singled out by respondents as their most serious nonlawyer competitors. A large number complained that banks draw up wills (often for nothing) and trusts, handle estates, and, in addition, advise people against seeking legal counsel.

That's one objection I have of the bar association. They should take an active part in stopping the soliciting of banks and trust companies who say you needn't consult your own lawyer. Other states don't allow that—pamphlets the banks send: "When have you last revised your will?" and so on. My experiences with banks are sorry. I'm amazed at the number of people—ten people I've had who want me to look over a will prepared for them by the —————— Bank, or the —————— [a trust company]. And they hang on to the executed will. That might prevent a man from altering his will. There's a lot of encroachment, most from banks and trust companies. And the advice they give is only as good as the individual they employ. Mostly in the fields of wills, estates, and trusts. These people concern me most. (39)

When a bank will prepare a will for free, naming the bank as trustee, that hurts. (12)

> The banks, although they advertise "See a lawyer," in fact take over estate work, write wills and trusts. (84)

Where a will is in existence it is offered for probate after the testator's death by sending a petition to the clerk of the County Probate Court with the will attached. In the petition there will also be a request that an executor be appointed by the court (usually the one named in the will) to administer the estate. Where there is no will, and the estate is large enough, a petition will also be filed to appoint an administrator. Where the estate is small, it is not uncommon for the lawyer to distribute the assets himself without benefit of probate. One lawyer had $2,700 in a special account representing the estate of a deceased Chinese client:

> I'll distribute it myself. I'll ascertain who is alive in China. It won't go through the probate court. (41)

Two or three others mentioned that they were holding estate funds in their possession, but it was not clear if they were administering these estates through probate.

After an executor or administrator has been appointed, an inventory of the assets of the estate must be filed with the court. Thereafter, payments must be made on valid claims against the estate, including the expenses of administration and federal and state estate and inheritance taxes. The latter may involve getting an assessment of properties and possible negotiations with the Attorney General's Office or hearings before the state inheritance tax division. Finally, disbursements must be made and a final accounting submitted to the court. As has been mentioned, where a bank or trust company is involved as executor, many of these matters are handled by it. Nevertheless, the lawyer will have to keep checking the file to see that certain matters are taken care of; he may have to prepare an inventory, draft the final accounts for closing the estate, and see that it is filed properly, handle the sale of securities or other assets, prepare and file the tax returns, and, of course, be present in court at the hearing to admit the will for probate and on other procedural matters.

Most lawyers appear to get will-probate-estate business through informal contacts, from relatives, friends, and acquaintances; one lawyer pointed out that the older you get the bigger the estates you get to handle. Some, as we have seen, have contacts with banks and trust companies, and a few indicated that they got work from undertakers: "That's a natural," one lawyer noted, "they're a good source—I send them business in return." (34)

CRIMINAL

The type of criminal practice in which those lawyers handling only an occasional criminal matter are engaged generally centers around the local police court or the traffic court, and, in most instances, is an incident of an ethnic, neighborhood-oriented practice. Most of these lawyers also handle some divorce matters, and the relationship between police court and divorce practice mentioned in the preceding section is further illustrated in the following quotation:

> I handle some small criminal cases. This year I had one case, an indictment in felony court, a bench trial. The rest

> would be either police court—up to the preliminary hearing, getting charges reduced to misdemeanors, and so on—assault and battery, domestic problems, mostly drunks and disorderlies, assaults, etc. Neighborhood stuff. So many domestic relations cases come out of the police court; after representing them in the police court, you get them dismissed for divorce. (47)

One of the neighborhood lawyers said he tried to stay away from this kind of practice:

> I don't like to appear in police court, in that field—over-the-fence argument, husband beats wife and that sort of thing. If a person needs a defense, well, the time you spend in police courts just can't be compensated, and the people who get into police courts you're not going to get any business from. (19)

The most frequently mentioned traffic court matter was the defense of drunken driving charges. One respondent said that he generally took such cases as an accommodation for a client:

> I've handled six drunken driving matters in the past year, as an accommodation. I'm sort of an expert in trying drunken driving suits. (38)

Another lawyer went into some detail on how such matters are handled:

> . . . Before ———'s [a county official] directive was handed down you could get the charge [of drunken driving] changed—not a fix exactly—to reckless. Now you can't. That puts a greater duty, a burden on the court to determine the truthfulness of the arresting officer, because that's

the only evidence. If he stops you on the outer drive early in the morning and you've had a few drinks, and he says you're driving under the influence—and if he asks you to take a drink test and you do, you're crazy, because the cop has to justify his arrest, and you can't cross-examine the machine. If you're found at the side of the road, and no one saw you driving, you defend by saying that in spite of the showing, you weren't driving. I have one now. I can beat this one on the facts: No one saw you drive the car, and so on.

Interviewer: How many of these cases do you have?

Respondent: Nothing in excess; if you do, you're prone to becoming a political butt, subject to every copper and politician out for a handout. If they don't see you all the time, you're still a general practitioner. I don't want all of them; I'd be wearing out my welcome with the judge, the clerks, and so on. You need help, and you have to pay if you do it too often. I take the cases I can prove, no tough ones—not that I'm an honorable practitioner. There's a way of handling these things. A man's not particularly anxious to put a guy in jail—if he's an honorable citizen, and not doing anything—but under the new law a cop is potentially worth—a millionaire. (30)

Of the two specialists in the criminal field, one does police court work and the other handles more serious cases. Let us briefly consider the practice of each. The first lawyer had recently retired as an Assistant State's Attorney because of illness and at the time I interviewed him worked only in the morning picking up cases at a local police court:

Every day since I've been at a curtailed practice, I'm at the ——— Court, and I always hope to be back here by noon. I never liked it, my physical condition being what it is, but I have no choice. People come into these neighborhood courts—they have no foresight—without a lawyer and needing one. They learn to expect one around, however. Yesterday it was nothing, I was back here at 10:30. . . . It was the first thing I started doing, at the suggestion of my friends. They said: "You don't live far away, it'll be good for you, won't think of yourself for a while, it's short, just two-three hours a day, and sometimes you pick up a decent buck!" The bondsmen, sometimes they come in and ask us to take a case—there are two or three of us there.

Most of his work comes from bondsmen, policemen, a minister friend, and occasionally from a local precinct captain:

I could get more if I were in the full-time practice—work closely with bondsmen, police, precinct captains. If I would re-establish myself full time, I'd do it that way and get back full flood in three months.

What distinguishes this lawyer from others handling only occasional police court matters is the necessity in his case of maintaining more or less regular sources of business, which means he has to give something to the bondsmen and precinct captains, even though he has a reputation in the neighborhood and is known politically because of his previous activities. The intense competition for business at this level of criminal practice makes such payments a virtual necessity:

Interviewer: Is there a problem of competition from other lawyers in getting business?
Respondent: Oh, yes, always has been in all fields, particularly in the criminal field. For example, a man I know was arrested in the last half hour. He gets word out to a

relative to get me. A couple of hours elapse—he may have a half dozen cards in his pocket. Bondsmen and policemen are responsible for that. Or I'll talk about a case with a person and he'll say the other fellow will do it for less. There's always shopping around in the criminal field. (76)

The other specialist handles more serious cases in both state and federal courts. At the time of the interview he had three cases pending on the criminal side of the federal court: income tax violation, sale of narcotics, and mail fraud. Three out of four of his cases are in the state felony courts. On the average, he puts in two hours a day in court, and the rest of his day is spent either at the State's Attorney's Office or in his own office. Asked to describe his clientele, he replied:

> All the way from exposers to bank robbers, anything and everything. Mostly working class. (63)

Half his criminal clients come to him through bondsmen, and he generally has to give them a part of his fee: "Many times they participate with you—we'll all get disbarred. But no Christmas presents." The rest come in from "other criminals you've defended, policemen 20 per cent, and other lawyers 5 per cent."

COLLECTIONS

Most of the lawyers handling an occasional collection matter are generally lower-level real estate, personal injury, divorce, or business-corporate specialists. An indication of how such matters are handled by these lawyers may be seen in the following:

> I got a phone call from attorney ———, concerning a case in which I had caused a levy on an auto of his client who wanted the auto back. We agreed to a settlement on the thing. I agreed to meet him downtown at 3:30 at the bailiff's office to sign a release. . . . I wrote a letter advising a man that if he didn't return a down payment of $310 —on a furnace job he was unable to finance, couldn't go through with—we would take action in the State's Attorney's Office for fraudulently accepting money. (5)

> I sent out a couple of collection letters today. One is for a press repairing firm, the other a local grocery and market. Both are small claims. (47)

> Yesterday I straightened out a garnishment suit against a client. It involved making some phone calls. Now the question is whether or not the debtor wants to pay 50 cents on the dollar. (69)

Several upper-level business-corporate and real estate lawyers said that they handled some collection matters for their business clients. Not infrequently the corporate lawyer finds that part of his job in representing his corporate clients involves the handling of garnishment suits against the company's employees, partly as a service to the employees and partly to represent the company's interest in the matter. One lawyer said that he set aside a day a week for handling employees' problems. In addition, there will be other collection problems for the business client as such. One lawyer noted that he had just been involved in negotiating collections from subcontractors on behalf of a corporation he represents.

A few upper-level personal injury lawyers said that they handled collections for doctors as an accommodation without charging. It may be recalled that free legal services were mentioned as one method of inducing doctors to supply them with personal injury cases. Frequently a minor type of legal service, such as a collection, handling a traffic court matter, filing a tax return, etc., will be traded in a sense for favorable treatment in the future, either for a business source or an existing client.

One lawyer has a fairly sizable collections business that is largely an adjunct of his commercial finance company. His company is in the business of lending money to small businessmen, generally jobbers and wholesalers, on the collateral of their accounts receivable or inventories. If the borrower defaults, the respondent moves in, takes possession of the inventories or accounts receivable, and tries to liquidate or collect them. "We concentrate," he said, "on endeavoring to accomplish a fast and successful liquidation."

The more usual type of collections practice is exemplified by the only lawyer in the sample specializing in this field. Asked to describe his practice, he said:

> Other people say, "He's a collections lawyer." I don't. I'm as capable to handle a real estate problem as any other lawyer, or to set up a corporation, keep corporate minutes —I didn't forget.

Ninety per cent of his practice, however, is in collections, a good part of which comes from other lawyers:

> I do a lot of work for other lawyers—a lawyer's lawyer. A lot of lawyers can get judgments but can't collect. I come in then. . . . They come from all over, downtown, neigh-

borhood, big firms. One big firm gave me a bank from out of town to collect on a matter involving $300. They said it would cost them more to open a file, they didn't want any split fee. It's either firms or individuals, generally individuals. Most law firms have a collection department or hire a law clerk to do it and throw him the garbage. I handle all garbage.

Asked about his practice on referral fees, he replied:

I remit back a portion. It's individualized. A lawyer today gave me a $16,000 note to collect. I'm leery about it. That lawyer's no slouch—why did he turn it over to me? Well, on that my share will be two thirds rather than one half. . . . Some lawyers don't want their clients to know you're handling it—that's true most of the time.

Most of his business, however, comes directly from small retailers, collection agencies, or finance companies. Asked to describe his clients, he said:

Goofy bastards. Mine are mostly business houses, collection agencies, stores, and finance companies. Here's a file from ———— [an acceptance company], a credit clothes outfit, a lot of jewelers—dollar down places. Very few individuals, 75 per cent are business houses.
Interviewer: What per cent are Jewish?
Respondent: It's mixed. Anyone knows I can collect. You become recognized in the field. They don't look at the fact that I'm Jewish. About half are Jewish, I suppose.

Half of his time, he said, was given to court work, very little trial work, but preparing pleadings, appearances, motions, etc. A good deal of the time, he said, is spent with clients, mostly in his office. On further reflection, however, he noted:

Often you never see 'em at all. You get a call from ———
[a clothing company]. What's the deal? Send cards. We
have tickler cards in this business, and he'll send them in
later. You talk to the credit manager—you never see the
real manager. You don't prefer it this way—it's an im-
personal thing. They don't regard a collections man really
as their lawyer. . . . And I have to argue with clients.
They call you up, a guy calls up, there's a fellow working
at International Harvester, they want you to slap on a
garnishment—what plant? He didn't know. I can't find
him. I call the client and say, "Charge the account with
court costs"—and they don't like it.

Interviewer: Is there a problem of competition in getting business?

Respondent: Yes, in my field, more so than in others.
There are a lot of collection agencies who go out and get
the business, but I'm hamstrung by "ethics" from doing
the same thing—they generally turn it over to someone
they know, and if you're not connected with one of them
you can't get along. The main competition is from the
agencies and other lawyers. For example, someone calls,
I say my fee is 50 per cent and if no collection no charge—
you get a lot of dead-beat accounts. They'll say some other
lawyer will do it for a third, then you say, "I've got twenty-
two years' experience."

Interviewer: Is there much shopping around?

Respondent: They shop around. You find it very often
that they list with you and also five other guys—it's a lot of
trouble.

In commenting on his income, he stated:

Last few years—that's the peculiar part of the law practice—I haven't been doing so hot.

Interviewer: Under $4,000 a year?

Respondent: Yes. Though I have grossed $10,000 a year

—the last few years were bad. I have some business investments. (84)

This type of collections practice is ordinarily based on
a very large volume of small claims for credit houses and
collection agencies, with highly routinized procedures for
keeping accounts, preparing and filing garnishment pleadings, and so on. Many lawyers look down upon this kind
of work, sharing the view of the lawyer above that the collections lawyer handles "garbage." One lawyer was planning on moving to another suite because the lawyer who
shared his office operated a collections business. Another
lawyer, at the close of the interview, suggested that I speak
to an acquaintance in an office down the hall:

> I used to be in an office with him—a nice fellow—in col-
> lections. I couldn't stand it, tying up a guy's salary. They
> call you up and ask you how they're going to feed their
> family. "What do I feed my kids with?" they'd say. (94)

Within most areas of practice, as we have seen, there are
two distinct types of practitioners. If we now classify all
respondents as either upper or lower level [20] we find a
number of major differences between these two levels of
practice.

With respect to both office location and source of clients,
lower-level practitioners are anchored to a particular
neighborhood to a far greater extent than are upper-level
lawyers. Close to 30 per cent of the lower-level lawyers
maintain a neighborhood office and almost half draw a
fifth or more of their clients from their own neighborhood.
Lower-level lawyers also find themselves largely restricted
to an ethnic clientele of working-class individuals and
small businessmen. The services they perform for their

clients are basically those of a broker, bringing the client in touch with another lawyer, a real estate or insurance agent, bank, or some other private or public agency and possibly mediating between them.

Upper-level practitioners have moved considerably beyond a neighborhood, although not necessarily an ethnic, clientele. None has a neighborhood office, and only a few draw at all upon neighborhood sources for business. Those in the real estate and business-corporate areas represent fairly large corporate clients for which they perform more or less continuous services. Many of these lawyers have become intimately involved with their business clients, over half to the extent of going in on deals with them. The upper-level personal injury, tax, and divorce lawyers, on the other hand, have succeeded in developing regular *sources* of law business through arrangements with "suppliers," well over half relying heavily on referrals from other lawyers.

Because the mass production character of their practice allows them to standardize most technical aspects of their work, upper-level personal injury, tax, and divorce lawyers are somewhat less frequently called upon to perform high-level technical skills than are upper-level real estate and business-corporate lawyers. Far more important for these personal injury, tax, and divorce lawyers is the exercise of business-getting and institutional-manipulative skills, and it is to a large extent on these skills that their specialization rests.

Differences between these two levels of practice are also reflected in the extent to which lawyers expressed concern with the problem of competition. A little over 40 per cent of the lower-level practitioners said they felt there was a serious problem of competition from other lawyers in getting business, compared with less than 20 per cent of the upper-level lawyers. Lower-level personal injury, divorce, and general practitioners seemed to be most troubled; upper-level real estate and business-corporate lawyers were least troubled. Personal injury, moreover, was the area in which competition was said to be most aggravated, and was specifically mentioned by 40 per cent of the respondents.

Competition from nonlawyers, principally real estate brokers, banks, and savings and loan associations, was perceived as even a greater problem than competition from other lawyers. Although lower-level lawyers were again more concerned than upper-level lawyers, the difference between the two in this regard was smaller than it was with respect to perceived competition from other lawyers.

Finally, differences between the two levels are reflected in overhead costs and income. Overhead costs for upper-level lawyers are 75 per cent higher than those of lower-level lawyers, the upper-level real estate and business-corporate lawyers reporting the highest costs. Upper-level lawyers also reported incomes from the practice of law about 70 per cent higher than those of lower-level lawyers —a median annual income of $14,500 as compared with $8,500.

The reason why some respondents have been able to move beyond a lower-level type of practice will be examined in part in the next chapter when we take a closer look at the problem of getting business. In the last two chapters we shall consider how level of practice affects lawyers' ethics and the extent of their dissatisfaction with the practice of law.

NOTES

1. The distribution of the 67 respondents in independent private practice (see Appendix A, Section 2) by office location and size is as follows:

TABLE 16

Number of Lawyers in the Office	Office Location		
	Loop	Neighborhood	Total
One	7	7[a]	14
Two	7	0	7
Three	13	0	13
Four	14[b]	1	15
Five	7	0	7
Six plus	10	1[c]	11
Total	58	9	67

[a] Two have offices in their homes, and two are in real estate offices.

[b] Two also maintain neighborhood offices.

[c] This respondent has a law office in a building otherwise occupied by a savings and loan association. He also maintains a Loop office.

2. This includes the preparation of documents, principally pleadings, contracts, and leases, "going through a file" (periodic checking on the status of a particular matter or suit), and correspondence. Time devoted to writing legal briefs and memoranda is at a minimum for all but a very few respondents. Reading legal material either for "keeping up" or on research in connection with some matter at hand accounts for only a small fraction of the individual practitioner's working day—less than a half hour a day, on the average. And only 6 respondents specifically mentioned engaging in any legal research.

3. The most frequently mentioned courts are: the Superior Court of Cook County, the Circuit Court of Cook County (both are the trial courts of general jurisdiction in Cook County and their power and jurisdiction are identical), the Municipal Court of Chicago, the police and outlying magistrates' courts, and the Probate Court of Cook County. A good part of the time in court is apparently consumed in just "hanging around," waiting to be heard on motions and pleadings or to transact business with the clerks. While most individual practitioners spend at least some time in court, very few actually try cases: 9 respondents said that a third or more of their time was devoted to trial work, and only 3 said half or more of their time.

4. The most frequently mentioned local agencies are: the County Recorder's Office, the County Treasurer, the County Clerk, the County Assessor, the building and zoning department, the State's Attorney's Office, and the Board of Tax Appeals. State agencies were mentioned far less frequently, and the only federal agency mentioned at all frequently was the local office of the Bureau of Internal Revenue.

5. The eight areas of individual practice and the number of respondents devoting varying proportions of their time to each area is shown below:

TABLE 17

PROPORTION OF TIME IN THE AREA

Area of Practice	"Specialists" 30% or more	Some, less than 30%	None	Total
Real Estate	21	31	15	67
Business-Corporate	21	23	23	67
Personal Injury	14	29	24	67
Divorce	7	37	23	67
Will-Probate-Estate	6	51	10	67
Tax	5	28	34	67
Criminal	2	18	47	67
Collections	1	30	36	67

6. For legal requirements in the state of Illinois, see Illinois Business Corporation Act of 1933, Illinois Statutes, Chapter 32, Sections 157.46 to 157.51.

7. For discussion of the growth of title insurance and the role of the title company in real estate transactions, see Quintin Johnstone, "Title Insurance," *Yale Law Journal,* Vol. LXVI, No. 4 (February, 1957).

8. As a rule the Chicago Title and Trust Company will not issue the guarantee policy until after the closing, that is, until after the deed of conveyance has been recorded, since the buyer will want the policy issued in his name as owner. The buyer then is forced to rely on the opinion letter at the time of the closing.

9. Illinois Statutes, Chapter 120 (Revenue Act of 1939), Section 697, in particular. "Section 253 of the Revenue Act of 1872, as amended in 1881, remained the statutory basis for such [foreclosure] proceedings down to 1933. In the Depression period following 1929, the amount of tax delinquencies, particularly in Cook County, grew to almost fantastic amounts. A new and more drastic method of tax foreclosure was necessary." Editorial comment to Section 697 of the Revenue Act of 1939, Smith-Hurd Illinois Annotated Statutes. Statutory revisions took place in this area in 1933, 1935, and 1939.

"On tax foreclosures prior to 1940, it was possible to foreclose on *improved* property. The tax savings on such property were staggering, running into millions of dollars. Involved in such proceedings were many Loop properties where politicians worked hand in hand with speculators in effecting the best possible settlements.

"This was the first of the tax foreclosure scandals. Newspapers gave much publicity to the corruption in the processing of tax foreclosures on improved properties. It exhibited pictures of properties and statements showing settlements at ridiculous amounts. The result was the elimination of improved properties from tax foreclosures.

"Then followed wholesale foreclosures on vacant properties. Developers and speculators took advantage of this situation and also worked hand in hand with the politicians and their henchmen.

"In the middle 50's, an investigation by one of the local newspapers disclosed that the county was losing millions of dollars by reason of a failure in most cases to collect full penalties on unpaid taxes not included in the foreclosure. This resulted in a major tax scandal which was instrumental in electing a Republican State's Attorney and forcing a Democratic candidate for Governor to withdraw from the ticket.

"Tax foreclosures today [1962] are at a very low ebb since there is, at present, a very small percentage of delinquent tax items." (Letter from a Chicago lawyer not in the sample.)

10. This cut-off date has been changed by periodic amendments to the statute.

11. For relevant statutory provisions in Illinois, see Illinois Statutes, Chapter 120 (Revenue Act of 1939), Sections 510 to 550 (listing and assessment of real estate and personal property), and 575 to 606 (revision by assessing officers and Board of Review).

12. An investigation into the operations of the Cook County Assessor's Office was instituted in 1957 by U.S. Attorney Robert Tieken to determine whether income taxes had been paid by officials in the assessor's office on money allegedly received for "adjusting" assessments. "The investigation began after a secret coded ledger was found in the assessor's office which listed persons who had received favored tax treatment. . . . Witnesses have told the grand jury, it was reported, that some employees in the assessor's office have incomes in the six-figure bracket, more than 10 times their county salaries" (Chicago *Daily News,* Oct. 15, 1957). A *Daily News* editorial writer put the blame on Illinois' antiquated and unrealistic revenue laws: "What it demands is impossible. Nobody could afford to deposit money in a savings account or to own securities if this provision [relating to the taxation of personal property] was carried out literally. The taxes would exceed the interest or the dividends that could ordinarily be earned. The tax would confiscate part of the capital. . . . All officialdom, including the courts, connives at a violation of the state's fundamental law because that law is unreasonable and unenforcible. . . . When Mr. Tieken finishes his job, the public may finally be shocked sufficiently to revise the Constitution and put the assessing business on an honest and enforcible basis" (Oct. 16, 1957).

13. "The reporter who wanders through the ancient, dingy Cook County courthouse in Chicago is likely to find trials droning over accidents that took place from six to eight years ago. Recently a Chicago jury was pondering the case of ten-year-old Nancy Vernola who was hit by an automobile while riding a bicycle. By trial time Nancy was a young mother of nineteen and brought her six-week-old baby to court with her." Louis Banks, "The Crisis in the Courts," *Fortune,* December, 1961, p. 90.

Studies of court delay, particularly as this problem is affected by personal injury claims, have been undertaken at the University of

Chicago and Columbia Law Schools. Reports on research so far completed include: Zeisel, Kalven, and Buchholz, *Delay in the Court* (Boston: Little, Brown and Company, 1959); Rosenberg and Sovern, "Delay and the Dynamics of Personal Injury Litigation," *Columbia Law Review*, LXI (1959), 1115; Franklin, Chanin and Mark, "Accidents, Money and the Law: A Study of the Economics of Personal Injury Litigation," *Columbia Law Review*, LXI (1961), 1. For comparative statistics on court delay, see the annual reports (since 1953) of the Institute of Judicial Administration, New York University.

14. The Columbia studies indicate a very high correlation between size of recovery and age of claim (or suit), that is, the larger the amount recovered the greater the delay in settlement. Furthermore, their evidence indicates that large size causes delay, not that delay increases size of recovery (see Franklin, Chanin and Mark, *op. cit.*, p. 31).

15. It has been estimated that in New York City only 4 out of 10 personal injury claims ever result in suits, and only 2% are tried to judgment (see Franklin, Chanin and Mark, *op. cit.*, p. 10).

16. This lawyer's name, however, has appeared at least once to my knowledge in Irv Kupcinet's "gossip" column in the Chicago *Sun-Times.*

17. For an extremely illuminating discussion of the growing dilemmas of the divorce lawyer and of divorce practice generally, see F. B. McKinnon's unpublished manuscript, *Study of the Ethical Problems of Practicing Lawyers,* chapter entitled "Some Ethical Problems of Divorce Practice" (Harvard Law School project in progress).

18. Letter from the Rt. Rev. Msgr. Edward M. Burke, Chancellor of the Archdiocese of Chicago to F. B. McKinnon, May 25, 1954.

19. Lecture delivered by the Rt. Rev. Msgr. George J. Casey, May 5, 1944, in *Canon Law on Civil Action in Marriage Problems* (Chicago: Catholic Lawyers Guild of Chicago, 1944).

20. It will be recalled that only those lawyers specializing in the business-corporate, real estate, personal injury, and divorce areas have been divided into the two types of practitioners. The remaining respondents, including 5 with less than 30% of their practice in any given area, can also be classified by the degree of technical legal skill involved in their work. The resulting distribution of all 67 respondents by level and area of practice is shown here:

TABLE 18

DISTRIBUTION OF 67 RESPONDENTS BY LEVEL

AND AREA OF PRACTICE

Main Area of Practice	Level of Practice		
	Lower	Upper	Total
Real Estate, Business-Corporate	14[a]	18[b]	32
Personal Injury	7[c]	7[d]	14
Divorce	2	3	5
Tax	1	4	5
Criminal	1	1	2
Municipal	0	1	1
Collections	0	1	1
Litigation	0	1	1
General Practice	6[e]	0	6
Total	31	36	67

[a] Includes one respondent with 30% of his practice in divorce, and three with one third of their practice in will-probate-estate.

[b] Includes one respondent with 40% of his practice in tax foreclosure.

[c] Includes one respondent with 30% of his practice in will-probate-estate.

[d] Includes one respondent with half his practice in divorce.

[e] All but one of these respondents reported less than 30% of their practice in any given area; the remaining respondent had a little over 30% of his practice in the will-probate area.

3
Getting Business

A continuing problem for many individual practitioners is how to get business. In this chapter we will consider, first, the different ways in which the individual lawyer goes about trying to build up his practice and, second, the competitive problems he encounters in getting and keeping clients.

BUILDING UP A CLIENTELE

The young lawyer just starting out in practice probably looks first to his friends and relatives for clients. While some young lawyers have undoubtedly been helped in this way, most find it very difficult to build up a practice by relying principally on family sources.

Unfortunately, my father—he's the world's greatest guy, they threw away the mold when they made him—he hasn't been in a position to help financially. (6)

Several lawyers, moreover, said that they generally avoid family matters because relatives make the worst clients, the uniform complaint being that relatives are difficult to please and often unwilling to pay for services:

Family you can have. Most lawyers don't want family business. They expect you to work for little or nothing. They are unsatisfactory clients. (26)

I don't want business from relatives. If you lose, you're a bum; if you don't, then anybody could have done it—and in any event, they don't pay you. (3)

In almost all cases the individual lawyer has to go beyond the narrow familial circle in his search for clients. Some, particularly in the early years, turn to their own neighborhood. One lawyer, for example, who has lived all his life in the same area, when asked how he got his first clients replied:

They just walked in here. I was born and raised in the neighborhood. My family has been here 50 to 75 years— hell, we're known in the neighborhood. . . . Friends and acquaintances in the neighborhood, they recommend me. (19)

Another lawyer noted the significance of neighborhood contacts in his first years out of law school:

My drugstore contacts helped a great deal.
Interviewer: How?
Respondent: I told the customers, the neighbors, that I

was going to law school. From 1924 to 1932 I worked in one store. It was in a German neighborhood [on the Northwest side]. I got to know the families, and they knew me. The first matter I handled I did for a man in the neighborhood. "When you get out of law school I'm going to give you some business," he told me. And he did. (16)

Although a neighborhood practice may have advantages, it is generally felt to be a less desirable type of practice, in terms of both the prestige it affords and the income it provides. The undesirable status of the neighborhood practitioner is aptly delineated in the following remarks by the only respondent in this group who has been able to achieve a fair degree of financial and professional success:

There was one thing I was concerned with—practicing in a neighborhood location. I found it irksome that people assumed that the good lawyers are downtown. They put the neighborhood lawyers in the same class with the real estate agent, insurance broker, and so on. In practicing I stressed the professional nature of the service; I in no way got involved with real estate, insurance, etc., arrangements that so many neighborhood practitioners have. . . . I felt it was possible to practice in the neighborhood as well as on LaSalle Street. . . . People don't look at the neighborhood lawyer as on the same professional level as the lawyer in the Loop—but on the same level as other service people, real estate and insurance brokers, and similar types of nonprofessional categories. He's looked at more as a neighborhood businessman rather than as a professional. Doctors don't have that problem; you don't consider Loop doctors to be on a completely different level. (10)

Most respondents quite understandably seek contacts that will take them beyond both a neighborhood and family practice, and these contacts are said to be established primarily on the basis of organizational participation.

An important part of the folklore of the individual practitioner is the notion that the way to get business is to be active in organizations. Thus according to one lawyer:

> If you practice law you have to belong to a lot of organizations, you have to be a mixer. If you wait for clients to come to you, no matter what the Code of Ethics says . . . (57)

One of the younger lawyers, in response to the question of whether he had any strategy for getting business, stated:

> Get out of the house! Not by sitting at home. Get out and mingle. It's the old maxim, but it works. People don't knock at your door unless you're well known, then you have no worry. (25)

Some organizations are said to be more helpful than others:

> Frankly, if you belong where there's wealth around, it does you a lot of good if you can stand up and show you can talk, make friends. They say it's just as easy to marry a rich girl; well, it's just as easy to get into an organization where there's wealth. It helps to belong, helps immeasurably, especially for a younger man. If you become an officer—the friends you make there—it's very helpful. (93)

Similar views are expressed in the following:

> Other lawyers join a lot of organizations as a means of getting practice. I wasn't much of a joiner. You just go

around and impress people with your ability and personality. You join many organizations, professional, business, lodges, social clubs, country clubs, and politics, all designed to expand your circle of acquaintances on the theory that you are more likely to come in contact with people who need a lawyer. (9)

> *Respondent:* First you have to be known.
> *Interviewer:* By whom?
> *Respondent:* Potential clients.
> *Interviewer:* How do you get yourself known?
> *Respondent:* You work in various organizations, civic organizations, persons in those organizations say, "I know a budding young lawyer; he will handle it more inexpensively." (5)

> The main problem is to know a lot of people. Get contacts, be active in organizations of one kind or another. (26)

> You have to join organizations, make numerous contacts. (48)

Another lawyer put it quite simply: "Business comes as a result of exposure, contact and more contact."

A few lawyers in the sample have in fact found such participation to be a source of business. One of them commented:

> It certainly made me a lot of friends, individually and organization-wise. It hasn't hurt my practice. I've done charity work, but those who paid made up for the difference. (33)

Another lawyer just starting out was certain that participation would be a great help:

> I expect it to be. I intend to become quite active in all three organizations I belong to [a conservative synagogue,

the B'nai B'rith, and a bowling league sponsored by the B'nai B'rith]. (2)

Many, however, have had second thoughts about the value of organizational activity. "Some join organizations, but that's where the competition is," a young lawyer pointed out. "You're not the only lawyer in the Elks or the Legion. Ten per cent are lawyers, probably all looking for business." (17)

The saturation notion was voiced by a number of respondents:

> These organizations are loaded with lawyers. (35)

> Well, I would say this, in all honesty, most of my friends are active in the Temple and some get clients that way . . . but there are a lot of other lawyers in there too. (18)

Others feel that it isn't worth the effort, that the potentialities for business are far overrated and that you end up giving more than you get:

> I would like to have one tenth of what they believe in advance they're going to get. (56)

> I got some business at KAM [a Reform synagogue] but it doesn't compensate me for the dues I've paid and the contributions I've made. (3)

> In church for fifteen years I haven't made $300. Kiwanis —all give and no get. (4)

> I've gotten in, but it didn't help. I was told, "You should join." But I can't say one can join groups and expect to receive business. (83)

> I never bothered with them. I never felt I could get much out of it—you put more in it than you get out of it. (86)

> If you belong to organizations, they come to you and think they can get it cheaper. . . . And it costs you to belong. (22)

> I've had Masons, Elks, etc., solicit me. I'm a Mason—but a lawyer already in there represents the organization . . . and when matters come up they refer it to regular lawyers in the lodge. (62)

Several were even disdainful of getting business in this manner, and one or two of the younger men who have felt the pressure to join said that they would prefer to spend that time at home with their families.

Regardless of these reservations, however, there is little doubt that the theory that you build up your practice through organizational participation is widely circulated among individual practitioners and is apparently widely acted upon.

Practically all the lawyers I interviewed are members of one or more nonprofessional organizations, and two out of three are active participators in these organizations. Those respondents more recently admitted to practice, as might be expected, are more likely to be active than those who have been in practice longer.[1]

While organizational participation may conceivably bring the individual practitioner into contact with a wider circle of potential clients, whether it does in fact will depend on the type of organization in which he is active. The organizations to which most (four out of five) individual lawyers belong are ethnic or religious in character —churches and synagogues, veteran and fraternal (Jewish War Veterans, B'nai B'rith, Knights of Columbus, and so on), and educational, recreational, action and defense groups (Jewish Community Centers, Young Men's Jewish

Council, NAACP, Polish Roman Catholic Union, Holy Name Society, Catholic Interracial Council, Zionist organizations, and many others). Substantially fewer respondents belong to general civic and community groups, veteran and fraternal groups (Masons, VFW, American Legion, and so on), and various clubs and alumni associations. Of those respondents who participate actively in these various organizations, close to half are active exclusively in ethnic or religious organizations, and more than four out of five are active in ethno-religious and/or general veteran and fraternal groups. As far as these latter organizations are concerned, active participation in them, far from guaranteeing a successful practice, may very well increase the difficulties lawyers have in moving beyond a restricted lower-level type of practice. Thus respondents who are active in ethno-religious and/or general veteran and fraternal groups are somewhat *less* likely to have an upper-level practice than those who are not active in such groups.[2] The only respondents who appear to have benefited substantially from organizational activity are those few (seven respondents) who participate exclusively in general civic, community, and similar groups, all but one of whom are upper-level lawyers. Over-all, however, there is no relationship between organizational participation and level of practice.[3]

This quite evident restriction on the type of organization in which the individual practitioner is likely to be active is undoubtedly a reflection of his more general dependence on ethnic and religious ties for building up his practice. Over half the respondents acknowledged that at least 50 per cent of their clients were drawn from either their own or some other ethno-religious group, and almost a third reported that 50 per cent or more of their clients were drawn from their *own* ethno-religious group.

Although he is often dependent upon ethno-religious ties for building up and maintaining his practice, the individual practitioner is generally unwilling to be identified as an ethnic-group lawyer: close to 80 per cent denied *any* such identification, over 20 per cent refusing on principle (occasionally quite vehemently) to be so identified.[4]

The individual practitioner's unwillingness to be identified as an ethnic-group lawyer reflects in part his aversion to being identified with a particular lawyer stereotype. Several Jewish lawyers, for example, remarked that the term "Jewish lawyer" was commonly used by clients, and a number recalled instances when a non-Jewish client came to them saying that he had done so precisely because he wanted a Jewish lawyer, or that the other side had a Jewish lawyer and he thought that he should have one, too. In the clients' view, this meant a smarter, cleverer, more aggressive lawyer.

> Among the foreign born, the lower grade, some of them say, "I want a Jewish lawyer, they're cleverer, smarter— innate shrewdness." Of course, that's not true. (11)

> Certain clients want to go to a "smart Jewish lawyer." (14)

> I have clients that use it [the term "Jewish lawyer"]. A divorce client came to me because I'm a Jewish lawyer —she wasn't Jewish. It carries a certain connotation. I asked her what it meant, she said it means more aggressive. I guess it can go in reverse. (29)

Although the Jewish lawyer may stand to benefit from such a view, most are not entirely pleased or flattered by it.

That there may also be a stereotype of the Polish lawyer is indicated in the answer of a lawyer of Polish descent to the question as to whether he considered himself to be a Polish lawyer:

> No [quite flatly]. You go along Ashland, Chicago, Milwaukee avenues—there's a Polish bar! I look at myself as an American. (19)

What these lawyers seem to be trying to avoid more, however, than a particular ethnic stereotype is the label of an ethnic-group lawyer as such, and the low status this implies. The generally low prestige attached to an ethnic practice rests not only on the fact that it is limited to particular ethno-religious groups but, even more important, on the fact that it is limited largely to individuals in a lower (if not the lowest) economic stratum of these groups.

In spite of his unwillingness to be identified as an ethnic-group lawyer, the individual practitioner is led, as we have seen, to exploit or take advantage of these ties as a source of business and as a way of building up his practice. This presents him with a serious dilemma, for the more ambitious he is the more he seeks to go beyond the narrow confines of an ethnic practice, the more he is forced to rely on the very ties he is seeking to avoid. Caught in this dilemma, some respondents have taken curiously contradictory positions—at one point acknowledging that a substantial proportion of their clients is drawn from their own ethno-religious group, while at another refusing to be identified as ethnic lawyers, precisely on the ground that their clientele is *not* derived from their own ethno-religious group.

Political activity, like other types of organizational participation, is primarily viewed as another means of expanding one's circle of contacts and as a necessary expedient in building up one's practice. Hardly any respondents appear to have become politically active with the idea of going into politics as a career. Their aim is rather to bolster their legal practice. Even those who are looking for political appointments (to the State's Attorney's or Corporation Counsel's Office, or to some other local government legal department) are essentially in the market for temporary or part-time positions as a supplement to their private practice. The same can be said about appointments as receivers, guardians *ad litem,* and masters in chancery.

Political activity for the individual practitioner is usually confined to the local ward and is most likely to occur during the first years in practice. Of those who are active politically, most are precinct captains, although some hold less formal or more temporary positions.

Unlike participation in the B'nai B'rith or the American Legion, being active in the local precinct organization does seem to have a beneficial effect on the individual lawyer's practice. Thus close to two out of three respondents active in local politics have achieved an upper-level practice, compared to half of those who are not active.[5]

The utility of political participation for the individual lawyer is not only limited to the realm of business-getting; equally important is its presumed function of enhancing his effectiveness in handling legal business, particularly in the local courts and agencies. Close to half the respondents strongly emphasized the importance of political connections in this regard,[6] and the necessity, especially for the younger lawyer, for being active in politics. These lawyers argue that everything is determined by political connections, that with such connections a good many of your problems are solved, and that without them you have two strikes against you.

Any lawyer who wants to make a reputation for himself joins organizations, helps him to get business . . . and the quicker he joins a political organization the better off he is. It is important for a lawyer who is practicing to know as many politicians as he can. Clients are only interested in results and politicians can get the results—zoning changes and matters controlled by an alderman—you have to approach them properly in the language they understand. (26)

A phone call to a judge can change the whole course of a lawsuit—or to the right individual. It's not what you know or what the law is, but who you know—especially in the Municipal Court in Chicago. If you know a politician who has pull there, you can get what you want. It's there, not only in the Municipal Court but in the Superior Court and the Circuit Court. You can go in on a matter, you have the law with you, and before you know it you're out in left field. If a client asks you about a particular problem, you read the cases and you get the decisions but in the courtroom it's not that way.

Interviewer: How have your connections worked?

Respondent: In the ordinary neighborhood, something happens, in any matter. The precinct captain or ward politician—he checks and sees if he knows the judge, or somebody he knows. It all depends on how much influence you can build up. The most damned discouraging thing, one matter [a divorce involving custody and property rights], it was argued for forty minutes. We had the law with us, cited cases, then the judge gets a phone call— he goes off the bench, and when he gets back he cuts the argument and, without saying why, rules for the other side. A most disheartening experience in the practice of law. I didn't know what hit me. . . . Then it's not the practice of law but who you know. Individual practice is a hard practice and rough, it's really a rough deal. (17)

The potential clientele available to most individual practitioners—in spite of and in part even because of his organizational and political participation—tends to be restricted to the same socioeconomic or ethnic stratum from which he comes.[7] In some cases it may even be further limited to a particular neighborhood or locality. Given this limited range of potential law business, the individual practitioner, and particularly the one just starting out, sees his only real chance for building up a successful practice in establishing special arrangements with individuals or groups in a position to supply or "feed" him with a relatively constant flow of business.

One obvious constant source of business is the large corporate client; but, as we have seen, only very few individual practitioners have corporate clients of any real size, and often they may receive only a part of the corporation's legal business. Cut off from this source, the individual practitioner turns to a rather special type of person who, by virtue of a variety of circumstances, is in a peculiarly advantageous or sensitive position for identifying and channeling potential legal business to the lawyer. Such a person becomes, in a sense, the broker between lawyer and client. The problem for the lawyer, then, is to make himself known and visible to the broker. The broker may be another lawyer, an accountant, a real estate or insurance broker or agent, a building contractor, a doctor, policeman, bondsman, precinct captain, garage mechanic, minister, undertaker, plant personnel director, foreman, etc. Several lawyers in the sample were quite candid as to the necessity for taking positive steps in this direction:

> A fellow has to have a key, chart his course. . . . You need some connections to get started. A firm feeds you business. If you're alone you must tie up with a policeman if you go into criminal practice; if probate, tie up with a minister or undertaker (they know people who die, or likely estates).
> *Interviewer:* Were you helped in that way?
> *Respondent:* From my church, the minister I had gone to high school with, I got business there—divorces, some criminal work, those fellows get into trouble too. I got my most successful criminal cases out of the church. (76)

Later in the interview he indicated that he had some misgivings about such practices, but he recognized their importance, especially for the young lawyer starting out:

> At the outset, if he wants to know how to get business—if he likes criminal work, he has to tie up with a policeman, bondsman; as simple as asking for business: "Look, fellow, I'm practicing law, here's my card," and you have to give him half of your fee. I never developed it that way. I frequently gave half of my fee, but it's not fair to me or the client. If a case is worth $100, it's worth it without padding. It's unfair for me to give $50, then I have to charge $150, or lie to the policeman, tell him I got but $50—and then he finds out. I've had policemen come to me: "I like the way you work." I take 'em but . . . One, for example, in the last six months (it can be lucrative; there's a lawyer lives at [a South Side address], does a lot of criminal work that way. Six years out and he drives a Cadillac.) He says: "give me your card." He says, "will you go out at night?"

I used to—I said *no* to the policeman. If a young fellow is in a hurry—and they frequently are, two or three kids on his neck—he might have to do it. But he should get away from it as quickly as he can, and he will by being honest and persevering. . . . The client knows that you've done a good job. He'll recommend you to someone else, and in three years you can forget about policemen.

A young lawyer just out of the State's Attorney's Office listed the sources of criminal practice in one short sentence:

All your criminal business comes from bondsmen, other criminals you've defended, policemen, and other lawyers. (66)

Personal injury and divorce have their special sources also:

I got PI cases through runners. They give you some rotten cases, though, the good ones they gave to the experienced lawyers. . . . I did a lot of divorce too which I got from rather dubious sources—waitresses in restaurants, B girls.
Interviewer: What advice would you have for a young lawyer just starting out?
Respondent: Go ask him what connections he has for bringing in business—unless he is a genius. The big fellows go to the big law firms; you get just individuals, unless you got chasers and doctors working for you—there's nothing like personal injury, it's the quickest dollar—you run like hell, send the good ones to trial and sit there and negotiate the rest. We had a chaser here as president of the club [respondent's town club]. He was a nice guy. (35)

Several have made important contacts through auto dealers:

> *Interviewer:* How did you get into sales tax work?
> *Respondent:* While I was in ———'s [a former State's Attorney] office I was invited to address a meeting of a used car dealers' association. They were impressed and asked me to become attorney for the association. I learned that the Illinois sales tax was a pressing problem. I started to read and acquire some suits. One was a $50,000 sales tax case. I got him out for $8,000—it started to grow since then. (55)

> I was considered a qualified practitioner in auto financing . . . commercial problems of collections, repossession of property, legal problems of securing property seized by authorities, and auto collections. . . . I had quite a few acquaintances among dealers, and a relative is a GM dealer. He recommended me to the GM Acceptance Corporation—their finance affiliate in Chicago—in connection with doing property repossession and collection work. (11)

Accountants may sometimes be a source of business:

> My first clients were from friends and acquaintances, referral business. I knew one or two accountants—they referred the legal business of their clients. (48)

An "in" with an insurance company or broker can result in subrogation or personal injury matters:

> I had a lot of friends—I couldn't get a nickel's worth without friendship—in the insurance business. They sent me suits to defend, and some plaintiff's business. . . . There's this fellow, an insurance broker, he sends me business; there are about ten like him, makes up 50 per cent of my business. They send me mainly plaintiff's work. (42)

Another lawyer had made an important contact with an Italian insurance broker who ultimately supplied him directly or indirectly with most of his practice.

> *Interviewer:* How did you meet this broker?
>
> *Respondent:* I once had a matter with a man who was insured by his office. An Italian, hurt in an accident, had a claim against a colored man who had no insurance. I was just getting started then on my own. I was able to persuade this man to borrow $100; I prevailed upon him to do it. I negotiated with the Italian, and he said he would have to consult with his insurance broker before signing any papers. Well, I went over to see the insurance broker, and he said: "How did you ever manage to get any money in this case? You must be a very ambitious man," and so on. And he said he would turn over some matters to me. The first case I had from him, I raised some money from a guy without insurance—and from then on . . . I also handle their other work—they have assets, make loans. And I do personal work for them—they call me for advice.
>
> *Interviewer:* At what point does he send work to you?
>
> *Respondent:* It's characteristic of insurance brokers in local neighborhoods, with a foreign element (not of brokers downtown), these poor people are very clannish, they don't go downtown—when they pay insurance premiums they think they should get free legal service, they expect their broker to send a letter out, and so on. And they do it as an accommodation—it's not really practicing law. Sometimes they get results, and if they don't they send it to me. A lot of these people don't want to pay attorney's fees. . . . These Italian people send me members of their families. (44)

The same broker put him in contact with a downtown insurance agency that helped him line up with an insurance company:

They had a lawyer they weren't satisfied with, and this particular Italian broker, he placed insurance through this agency, he spoke to me about it. I waited two years. This Italian broker places insurance policies through various agencies—they're all after him. This downtown group, an Irish group, they are agents for twelve or thirteen insurance companies. Well, this agency downtown, they line me up with this company, they said, "We place so much business with this company, you give business to this lawyer."

An Irish lawyer made a fortunate contact with the Polish owner of a large lumber company who not only gave him a lot of his own business but recommended him to a number of contractors he had dealings with:

Here's an interesting bit of folklore concerning the way I got ——— as a client. I called him up one day. I wanted to know where a certain contractor was doing work. I said, "Let me speak to Mr. ———." I pronounced his name correctly. Well, he wanted to know how an Irishman could pronounce a Polish name so well. I was the first non-Pole ever to pronounce it corectly. I said that means the month of ———. Well, he told me that a fellow had stopped payment on a check and that I should come and take care of it. He skyrocketed from a small yard to three big yards in the city. He's dead now. His brother married a lawyer's sister, and now I get the small stuff, what's tough—lien matters. (18)

A lawyer who spends most of his time in divorce work pointed out that an important source of business grew out of the contacts he had made with baseball players:

A girl came to me about a fracas with one of the Cub players. I sued him. Then it's like steppingstones, one contact leads to another. I always had many celebrities among my friends. I was in Salt Lake City—I was an intelligence officer in the army. I had to speak to all the new people there. When the European war was over they had a morale problem with the boys who were being shipped to the Asiatic theater. Well, they were shipping a lot of celebrities over there and they all went through Salt Lake City. I saw them all. I had to tell them to avoid all publicity and so on. These were baseball players, and so on. I retained those friendships that I made through that. I've known Howard Pollet since 1944, and I know Rocky Marciano and Dee Fondy, and Walter Dropo is one my closest friends, and he introduced me to the Harshmans, Pierces, and so it goes. (38)

Referrals from other lawyers constitute a major source of business for at least some respondents. Personal injury matters are most frequently referred; however, local tax, divorce, and criminal matters also were mentioned. Matters referred within a law office suite rarely account for more than a very small percentage of the individual lawyer's income. Only four respondents said that they had received matters from other lawyers in their suite that accounted for as much as 10 per cent of their law business. Much more important are referrals from lawyers outside the suite. Almost a third of the respondents indicated that matters referred to them in this fashion accounted for 10 per cent or more of their law business; almost a fifth said they accounted for a half or more of their practice. Referrals from lawyers outside the suite generally come from other individual practitioners or from lawyers in the smaller firms; only four mentioned that they received matters from the larger firms.

THE PROBLEM OF COMPETITION

In his struggle to build up and maintain his practice, the individual lawyer faces fairly stiff competition both from laymen and from other lawyers.

Lay competition. Competition from laymen in providing legal services is found in many areas of practice, but most particularly in the real estate, business-corporate, and will-probate-estate fields.[8] Just how extensive this encroachment is cannot be known on the basis of the evidence at hand, but it is probably not unreasonable to conclude that at least in certain areas individual lawyers are called upon far less frequently than laymen to handle what are ostensibly legal problems. What lies behind this state of affairs? Why is it that the domain of the individual practitioner has been so peculiarly prone to encroachment by lay competitors?

In practically all areas of practice—but principally in the real estate, business-corporate, and will-probate-estate fields—certain institutions or occupational groups perform critical functions with regard to the various matters or transactions involved. In the area of real estate closings, the real estate broker performs the important function of bringing buyer and seller together, the savings and loan association of providing financing, the title and abstract company of performing title searches and providing the all-important title guarantee insurance. Also in handling the affairs of the small businessman, accountants, and to some extent bookkeepers, are employed to keep a check on the books, financial records, and accounts of the business; and in administering estates, banks and trust companies are frequently called upon to act as executors. In each of these instances there is a tendency for the person or agency in question to extend and enlarge upon the facilities and services it offers, and because of the very close connection between its "legitimate" functions (some of which, as in the case of the abstract and title company, already overlap with legal services) and those traditionally performed by lawyers, encroachment seems to be almost inevitable. This extension of functions seems to be facilitated by the following factors:

1. Rationality, convenience, and efficiency.—The types of matters that have been taken over by lay groups and institutions are generally the less complicated matters or transactions involving a great deal of paper work—preparation and execution of documents—which when handled on a large volume basis can be formalized and standardized to a greater extent than would be possible for most individual practitioners. A savings and loan association or bank, for example, by virtue of the large number of closings or estates it is able to process, can develop more highly rational and efficient procedures and forms for handling the relevant routine legal aspects of a transaction than many individual lawyers. In speaking of the common characteristics of "encroaching" lay institutions, Karl Llewellyn said:

> They are specialists: each has worked out machinery for handling with maximum use of patterns, forms, routine, and concentration of expensive executive decision, *a semi-mass production of legal transactions or legal services* in a very limited field. . . . A title company simply can more effectively gather records than the ordinary lawyer can; and over the years it *can* therefore organize and do a job both more quickly, more effectively and more cheaply; it

can issue insurance which the ordinary lawyer cannot, against its own error or negligence. It offers a better social machinery for the job.[9]

There is an additional convenience to the client in having all phases of a transaction taken care of for him by one agency or by his broker or accountant, and these people are in the advantageous position of being able to offer the client a package deal.

2. Balance of skills and power.—The lay organization or individual quite often is not only able to provide a more efficient service but is sometimes in a position to command and apply a greater degree of technical skill than is possible for many individual practitioners. Accountants and estate planners, for example, frequently have a more comprehensive knowledge of tax law and procedures than do most individual lawyers. Furthermore, as we have seen in connection with the savings and loan association, the lay agency, because it is often in a stronger economic position, can insist upon handing both legal and nonlegal aspects of a matter.

3. Visibility.—Lay agencies, as a general rule, are in a far better position than are individual lawyers to make themselves and their services known to prospective clients. The lay agency has the advantage of its size, the fact that it can advertise, and that it provides a service that is generally recognized as indispensable. The individual practitioner is generally less well known by prospective clients, is prohibited by the Canons of Ethics from advertising in any direct fashion, and the services he offers are usually not thought of as indispensable.

4. Price.—The lay agency is in a position to charge far less for whatever legal services it may offer because of its

greater efficiency, its stronger economic position, and also because it is not dependent upon fees for such legal services as it may provide. In fact, it frequently can provide these services for little or nothing at all, as in the case of wills, estate planning, and so on.

Basic to the whole encroachment problem, and underlying the factors we have just considered, is the fact that the individual practitioner no longer has exclusive access to those institutions whose favorable action or the avoidance of whose unfavorable action is indispensable for a desired outcome with respect to the matters or controversies that he handles. Although lawyers still have a favored position in the courts, the court is today only one of many institutions and agencies of the character indicated above. With respect to practically all of the nonofficial agencies (banks, trust companies, insurance companies) and even some of the official ones (many of the administrative boards and local government offices), the lawyer finds that he is a member of only one of several service-oriented occupations that have access to and can deal effectively with these agencies. The situation is even further aggravated by the fact that many of these agencies will themselves deal directly with the prospective client.

The conditions just noted provide a striking contrast with the medical profession, where increasing centralization of essential "facilities" in the hospital has played a leading role in the virtual elimination of the problem of lay encroachment.

Competition from other lawyers. With respect to the problem of competition from other lawyers, let us consider the market for legal services in which the individual practitioner finds himself.

1. The demand for legal services.—The individual prac-

titioner has access to only a limited portion of the available demand for legal services, namely, those residual matters and clients that the large firms have not pre-empted, and that have not been encroached upon by lay organizations and agencies. Although the lower- and middle-income individuals and small businessmen whose problems these residual matters represent constitute the large bulk of the metropolitan population, the effective or articulate demand for legal services emanating from these groups is thought to be generally low and of an intermittent character.[10] There appears to be, first of all, a lack of awareness of the necessity for legal service or advice, particularly on the part of working-class families; and in addition, of those recognizing the need for such service, only a small percentage actually call upon a lawyer.[11] These people are also the least willing and the most apprehensive about obtaining a lawyer's services. For example, many believe that lawyers' services are prohibitive in cost. Typical of the attitude of many such people are the remarks of a Rochester respondent in the Koos study:

> What's the use of goin' to a lawyer—he'll only add a bill to what you owe or take away a lot of the money that's owed you, so you lose either way. Lawyers' bills add up every time you look at them—a poor man hasn't got a chance with a lawyer.[12]

Others feel that lawyers are not to be trusted, that they are crooks, unethical, interested only in their fees, and so on. These people are more likely to seek help from politicians, labor leaders, ministers or priests, or even neighborhood tavernkeepers or bartenders.[13]

2. An invisible market.—The market for legal services at the level of individual practice consists of individual

suppliers and consumers who are largely unknown and invisible to one another. Earlier in this chapter, in considering the problems of the individual practitioner in building up and maintaining a practice, it was pointed out that his efforts to expand his circle of acquaintances were, for the most part, specifically designed to increase his visibility to prospective clients or to establish contacts with those who already had such visibility. We found that a major theme running through many of the interviews was the great importance attached to being known, to making contacts. The common complaint voiced in answer to the question of what their major problems were in getting started was the lack of connections, the absence of anyone "feeding" them business. Similarly, the advice most generally offered to those just starting out in practice was to get known, establish contacts, get tied up with someone. The fact that a good many individual practitioners are unable to go beyond the narrow confines of an ethnic, neighborhood-oriented practice would seem to suggest that this problem persists, for even though a reputation may be established in a particular neighborhood or in certain ethnic islands, this is precisely the kind of identity and kind of practice that is least desired and one which the individual practitioner makes every effort to move beyond. The visibility problem persists also because of the small, nonrepetitive character of the matters to which he has access, requiring him continually to seek new clients.

3. The brokers.—In view of what we have just been saying, it is not surprising to find that a very important role is performed by those people we have termed business suppliers or brokers, for they are able to overcome both the low visibility of lawyer and client and the intermittent, "one-shot" character of the demand for legal services found

in so many areas of individual practice. Because of the crucial role played by the brokers, individual practitioners frequently find themselves competing not so much for clients as for brokers, who become, in a sense, their real clients. The services of the brokers involve a *quid pro quo* arrangement either in the form of a direct payment of money, securing a large fee (in the case of the doctor, and possibly others), free or low-cost legal services, or a reciprocal supply of business. Although brokers are found in every field of practice, they seem to be most prevalent in the personal injury, divorce, and criminal fields, and to a somewhat lesser degree in the local tax and real estate fields. Not all individual lawyers are equally successful in establishing contacts with brokers. The ability to establish contact with a resourceful broker depends on how much the lawyer can give in return, which turns to a large extent on his effectiveness in manipulating various agencies in effecting large savings, realizing large recoveries or settlements. Finally it should be noted that a strong bond of mutual dependence grows up between the lawyer and his broker. In the case of the less successful lawyer, however, the ties are weaker and there is generally a one-sided dependence on the broker that is frequently aggravated by the fact that the broker in some cases is also a lay competitor.

Those lawyers who are least involved with or have the weakest ties to brokers are apparently most directly in competition with other lawyers for clients. Being forced to compete for both clients and brokers, they are the ones who complain most about shopping around and price cutting.

> There is that [shopping around], yes. You'll find that mostly in divorce work. When they call you up and say,

"How much do you charge?" I tell them to come in, and if they say, "I can't make it," then I know they're shopping around. (19)

Yes, a lot of competition from unethical, unscrupulous lawyers. I would do a lot better if they were done away with, my practice would improve. (88)

N O T E S

1.

TABLE 19

Year Admitted to Practice	Per Cent Active Participators in Organizations	Number of Cases
1915–1926	50	(14)
1927–1940	66	(38)
1941–1957	80	(15)

Because of the small size of the sample, the relationships presented in this and other tables should be taken only as suggestive of those that might be found in a study with a larger sample from the same population.

2.

TABLE 20

Extent of Participation in Ethno-religious and/or General Veteran and Fraternal Organizations	Per Cent Upper Level	Number of Cases
Active	49	(37)
Inactive—nonmember	60	(30)

This relationship could be explained on the basis that the more successful a lawyer becomes the less need he has to be active in such organizations.

3.

TABLE 21

Extent of Participation in All Types of Organizations	*Per Cent Upper Level*	*Nmber of Cases*
Active	55	(44)
Inactive—nonmembers	52	(23)

4.

TABLE 22

Level of Identification (with own ethno-religious group or as an ethnic group lawyer)	*Per Cent*
Positive[a]	9
Moderately negative[b]	57
Strongly negative[c]	22
No data	12
Total	100
Number of cases	(67)

[a] All gave a "Yes" answer to the question "Do you consider yourself a Polish, Jewish, or Negro lawyer in any sense?"—and indicated they had been helped or had not been hindered in answer to the question on the influence of ethnic or religious ties on their practice.

[b] All but three gave a "No" answer, either generally or in terms of clientele, to the first question (3 answering "No" on principle) and all answered that they had been helped or not hindered by their religious or ethnic ties.

[c] All answered "No" on principle to the first question, some stating specifically that they did not want to be so identified, and either said that they had been hindered by their ethnic or religious ties or denied the significance of such ties in an aggressive manner.

5.

TABLE 23

Extent of Participation in Local Politics	Per Cent Upper Level	Number of Cases
Active	65	(17)
Not active	50	(50)

6.

TABLE 24

How important are political connections in the practice of law?	Per Cent
Very important; everything is determined by political connections	48
Important, but not crucial; more for some than others	24
Unimportant, overrated	19
No data	9
Total	100
Number of cases	(67)

7. Consistent with this conclusion is the finding that respondents from higher socioeconomic backgrounds are more likely to achieve an upper-level practice than those from lower socioeconomic backgrounds. Thus, lawyers whose fathers were either professionals or individual proprietors are more likely to be upper-level practitioners than those whose fathers were either white- or blue-collar workers.

TABLE 25

Class Origin	Per Cent Upper Level	Number of Cases
Professional and individual proprietor	65	(51)
White and blue collar	19	(16)

We also find that Jewish lawyers are more likely to be upper-level practitioners than non-Jewish lawyers.

TABLE 26

Religion	Per Cent Upper Level	Number of Cases
Jewish	64	(39)
Non-Jewish	39	(28)

Also, lawyers who have previously worked for a corporation or government legal department or as associates in large firms are more likely to be upper-level practitioners than those whose careers have been confined to the individual practitioner or small firm stratum of the bar.

TABLE 27

Career Scope	Per Cent Upper Level	Number of Cases
Wide	70	(23)
Narrow	45	(44)

While the small number of cases hardly permits more sophisticated analysis, the indications are that class background and career scope are more important than religion in determining level of practice. Thus among lawyers from higher class backgrounds non-Jewish lawyers have done as well as Jewish lawyers and both have benefited equally from a wider career scope. That religion should not be wholly ruled out, however, is suggested by the fact that, while non-Jewish lawyers from higher class backgrounds are more likely to have had a better law school training and a wider career scope than Jewish lawyers from higher class backgrounds, these non-Jewish lawyers have not done any better than their Jewish colleagues—roughly 2 out of 3 in both groups being upper-level practitioners. The fact that the non-Jewish lawyers have not done better may be the result either of the greater drive for success on the part of the Jewish lawyers, their greater ability, or their more extensive contacts with the world of small business—by virtue of family connections—or all three.

8. Competition from laymen arises also from the fact that many nonlawyers frequently act as intermediaries or brokers channeling legal business to lawyers, principally although by no means exclusively, in the personal injury field. In so far as many individual law-

yers themselves act as brokers they may have to compete with laymen for this type of business as well.

9. Karl N. Llewellyn, "The Bar's Troubles, and Poultices—and Cures?" *Law and Contemporary Problems,* V, No. 1 (1938), 112–113. See also Quintin Johnstone, "The Unauthorized Practice Controversy," *Kansas Law Review,* Vol. IV, No. 1 (October, 1955).

10. See Earl L. Koos, *The Family and the Law* (Rochester: Published in mimeographed form by the National Legal Aid Association, 1949); William H. Hale, "The Career Development of the Negro Lawyer in Chicago" (unpublished Ph.D. dissertation, University of Chicago, 1949), in which an attempt is made to determine the demand for the Negro lawyer's services; and George Buckner 2nd, "What Your Clients Think of You" (*Journal of the Missouri Bar,* XVII [1961], 468), a preliminary report of a study of laymen's attitudes toward lawyers based on interviews with a sample of over 350 Missourians. Buckner finds that, while 4 out of 5 laymen interviewed replied affirmatively to the question, "Have you ever gone to a lawyer for advice?" the users of lawyers average only 2 or 3 visits in five years (90% use lawyers' services less than 3 times in a 5-year period), compared to an average of 25 visits in five years for users of doctors. It should be noted that Buckner's sample excluded individuals earning $4,000 or less a year, so that the proportion of lawyer users and frequency of use for the total population must be considerably lower.

11. The principal exception is to be found in the personal injury area where, in view of the contingent fee arrangement and the notoriously high recoveries which lawyers sometimes obtain, the injured person feels he has more to gain and less to lose by going to a lawyer than not. Support for this conclusion comes from a study (for which I was research consultant) of automobile accident victims in New York City in which we found that 2 out of the 3 respondents (all of whom had reported receiving slight injuries) retained lawyers in an effort to recover for their losses and that lower socioeconomic status respondents were just as likely to retain a lawyer as higher socioeconomic status respondents. See Roger B. Hunting and Gloria S. Neuwirth, *Who Sues in New York City* (New York: Columbia University Press, 1962).

12. Koos, *op. cit.,* p. 10.

13. *Ibid.,* p. 6.

4

The Ethical Dilemmas of
Individual Practice

Between the official requirements of the Canons of Professional Ethics and the practical demands of individual practice there is often sharp conflict.[1] This conflict is apparent not only in the area of getting business, but also in dealings with courts and other official agencies and in relations with clients.

The solicitation problem. The conflict between the Canons on business-getting[2] and the realities of metropolitan practice have probably never been more forcefully or more clearly summarized than they were by Karl Llewellyn:

> The canons of ethics on business-getting are still built in terms of a town of twenty-five thousand (or, much more dubiously, even fifty thousand)—a town where reputation speaks itself from mouth to mouth, even on the other side of the railroad track; and reputation not only of the

oldster, but of the youngster. The youngster is watched when he hangs out his shingle; watched if he be a home-town boy, watched doubly if he be not. Word of law's work passes the time of day, along with sidetaking as between the Mathematics teacher and the High School principal. All the lawyers are known, and people who have legal work to do are moderately aware of it; and they have little difficulty in finding a lawyer of whose character, abilities, experience, yes, and fees, they can get some fair inkling ahead of time. And—no little item—where reputation works and counts, the overhead becomes materially less. "Front" that socially and personally is waste is peculiarly a privilege and an expense of the metropolitan lawyer.

Turn these same canons loose on a great city, and the results are devastating in proportion to its size. If a small client does not know to whom to go, he does his pondering through his brain—they over-reach, they over-charge, they are not even to be trusted. This means, in result, undone legal business. A-plenty. Or it means turning to some non-lawyer who undertakes to help out. Or it means chancing it. If the client chances it, he very truly chances it: the conditions of legal business make it no simple thing to reach into the grab-bag and pull out a lawyer who is able, experienced in the case at hand, not too taken up with other matters, and also reasonable in fee.[3]

The model for the present American Bar Association Canons of Ethics was the Code of Ethics adopted by the Alabama Bar Association in 1887, which was largely based upon Judge Sharswood's essay on professional ethics published in 1854.[4] Although those responsible for drafting the early Canons were not totally unaware of the special problems created by the large metropolitan environment, the image of the profession that is unmistakably conveyed by the Canons is of the small-town bar, consisting of lawyers who are highly visible not only to one another but to their prospective clientele, and who are capable, therefore, of attracting clients by establishing a reputation in the community as competent practitioners. These conditions, of course, do not exist today in the large metropolitan centers. The individual practitioner frequently finds himself in what we have termed an invisible market for legal services, and a market, furthermore, which is controlled to a large extent by encroaching lay agencies and business brokers. The nearly universal problem of gaining visibility, or of establishing contact with someone or some agency that has it, leads, as we have seen, to a skeptical, if not cynical view of the passive attitude toward business-getting implicit in the Canons. A large number of those in the sample, particularly in the early years although by no means confined to that stage in their careers, have assumed an aggressive attitude toward business-getting in violation of the spirit and frequently the letter of the Canons.

The problem of pay-offs and political influence. The use of personal influence and the trading or buying of favors in the courts or administrative agencies in order to obtain special treatment for a client is frowned upon by the Canons.[5] These prohibitions, however, make certain assumptions about the operation and personnel of the courts and administrative agencies and about the law that, like the rules restricting advertising and solicitation, appear to be at odds with actual metropolitan conditions. For a variety of reasons, the use of personal influence and the trading or buying of favors become an almost indispensable part of the individual lawyer's job, especially for those lawyers with more than occasional contact with the courts and administrative agencies.

In the course of handling clients' matters, there appear

to be two principal areas in which these problems are most acute. The first involves the routine processing of matters by clerks of the local courts and administrative offices. Here the lawyer is concerned with filing or checking through various documents, with having certain papers or documents certified or issued, with setting dates for hearings or appearances, or with having these dates changed. In order to secure prompt and efficient processing of these matters or to get a case or matter advanced or called ahead, to get a file in a hurry, or for minor conveniences or accommodations, the lawyer *must* take care of the clerk. Better than two out of three lawyers interviewed candidly admitted purchasing favors from clerks. In most instances, this meant giving a few dollars in the form of a tip or gratuity; almost a third also mentioned giving Christmas presents—box of cigars, carton of cigarettes, bottle of whisky—and several said they occasionally had to buy tickets of one kind or another. The lawyers with primarily a real estate or business-corporate practice, and who therefore have least contact with courts, account for most of those not mentioning the necessity for currying favor with the clerks. Several of these people pointed out specifically that such, however, had been their practice:

> I have no problem now as I did at the County Building. At Christmastime I had to hand out ten-dollar bills and boxes of cigars. (68)

> When I did a lot of court work I certainly gave gifts. (15)

> Years ago in the courts, when I was more active, I used to have more title work; around Christmastime, half a dozen to ten people would get gifts at the Chicago Title and Trust, and in the courts, about a dozen. But I've discontinued that. (85)

One lawyer who has drifted out of practice, giving most of his time now to his own investments, recalled the situation as it existed when he was more active in the courts:

> I don't do it any more. If it's hard to serve someone with a summons you give a few dollars to the bailiff; a few bucks to get a file to the clerk. . . . You can't get too much done without doing it. A clerk in the Municipal Court in the thirties got $1,800 a year—he has a little education, he has to be a high school graduate—$1,800 a year! Well, if you want something done in a hurry, he'll do it. (40)

Several lawyers more actively engaged in practice made some rather strong comments about the situation:

> Those officials are underpaid. Everybody's in there for what they can get. (11)

> It is essential to give money to get work done efficiently. (1)

> I maybe give them a buck to get on the docket earlier. I'm not naïve, but it doesn't sit well with me. Some lawyers carry dollar bills on them when they go into these offices. (8)

> *Interviewer:* Do you get favors from clerks?
> *Respondent:* If we do, we pay.
> *Interviewer:* At Christmastime too?
> *Respondent:* Any time. That's one of the vicious things about the practice. Not everyone does it, but those who don't, get lost. It's a difficult situation to overcome. (82)

> A clerk will call me ahead once in a while, help me with papers.
> *Interviewer:* Do you have to give them a couple of dollars?
> *Respondent:* A hell of a lot more than that, five, ten dollars.

Interviewer: You give them a gift at Christmas?
Respondent: Christmas is all year round. (37)

They all have their hands out, all the time. Jesus Christ, twenty-five, fifty dollars each time, clerks or bailiffs. Sometimes clerks can delay you for a month. (49)

I give breaks on ———— [product sold in his store]—not free. For everybody I come in contact with, even clients. It's very important. It's the reason I don't have a tough time others have. I must give away ———— by the thousands. Not money—that's a small amount. The other guy like me has to pay for these things. . . . The lawyer is a fawning specimen to begin with, he is continually asking for something, a beggar to begin with—he wants service from a clerk, a lowly clerk, and he begs for consideration from the court, he "prays" the court. (30)

The wide currency of such practices results in part from the sheer inefficiency characteristic of most of these offices, which are generally understaffed and invariably plagued with a large backlog of matters. Probably more significant, however, is the fact that almost all the personnel of these offices are political appointees grown accustomed to the favor system. And, finally, there is the tendency of a good many individual lawyers to compensate for their apparent insecurity, sense of inadequacy, and lack of confidence by acting like bigshots, passing out large tips and presents in order to ensure their being known by the clerks and other officials.

The pay-off and influence problem also arises from the application of certain local statutes and ordinances that are often grossly unrealistic, practically unenforceable, and inevitably coupled with a wide range of administrative discretion. These include most of the local tax laws (statutes dealing with tax foreclosure, personal property tax, real property tax), a large segment of municipal law (zoning ordinances, licensing statutes), and the divorce law (artificial limitations on or definition of the legal grounds for divorce). Under these conditions it is the lawyer who knows somebody in the State's Attorney's Office, in the Board of Zoning or Tax Appeals, in the Board of County Commissioners, or in a variety of other agencies and offices, or who is known by the judges, who will receive the more favorable interpretation or treatment, can expect a more advantageous adjustment or compromise, or will have his matter pushed through more expeditiously. Partly this is just a matter of paying off the right people and partly, because most of these officials are political appointees, of having the right political connections.

The fiduciary problem. A central requirement of the Canons is that the lawyer should adopt a trust or fiduciary relationship with his client, whose best interests he is supposed to promote, and that he deal directly and personally with the client without the intrusion of lay intermediaries.[6] From what we know of the nature of individual practice, however, there appear to be strong pressures forcing the lawyer-client relationship into two deviant forms in conflict with the requirements indicated above.

1. "Clients are expendable." In the case of those lawyers specializing in personal injury, local tax, collections, criminal, and to some extent divorce work, the relationship with the client, as we have seen, is generally mediated by a broker or business supplier who may be either another lawyer or a layman. In these fields of practice the lawyer is principally concerned with pleasing the broker or of winning his approval, more so than he is with satisfying the individual client. The source of business generally counts

for more than the client, especially where the client is unlikely to return or to send in other clients. The client is
then expendable; he can be exploited to the full. Under
these conditions, when a lawyer receives a client from a layman or a referring lawyer, he has not so much gained a
client as a piece of business, and his attitude is often that
of handling a particular piece of merchandise or of developing a volume of a certain kind of merchandise. If,
for example, as sometimes happens, a client who was orig-
inally referred by another lawyer returns, the question that
arises is not what obligation this lawyer owes in a professional sense to the client or to the lawyer who initially referred him, but how important the referring lawyer is as
a source of business. Where there is an opportunity or
prospect of getting more referrals, the lawyer will follow
the rule of notifying the referring lawyer (and offering him
part of the fee—generally a third) as an inducement to keep
sending him matters, otherwise he will not. Some lawyers
even extend this policy of notifying the referring lawyer to
the situation where the client refers another client, in
which case both the referring client and the lawyer may
get a cut:

> An ex-client referred me someone. He came [the ex-
> client] from a certain lawyer. Well, that lawyer still ap-
> pears on the file—that's my incentive to that lawyer, other-
> wise he'd be afraid of the repeat. A referral fee goes to the
> lawyer, and maybe also some to the client who referred
> it. (27)

Others won't go this far:

> If the client recommends someone else, then it's my
> client—I won't call the other lawyer. (8)

One reason for the different approach of these two lawyers is that the first is a specialist in personal injury, while the second is a general practitioner and less dependent on other lawyers for business. One young lawyer refused to do any more work for an older lawyer in his suite because where the repeat business was lucrative, the older lawyer insisted on taking complete charge of the matter.

> I used to get some referrals when I came in [to the office], but I asked him to stop—I didn't like the arrangement; they were still his clients and he charged only very small fees. I'd see the client, but he'd set small fees. He used it as an accommodation to his clients to get personal injury cases, so they'd feel warm to him and send him personal injury cases. I made peanuts, but if they came back and referred another case to me, that was to be his client and his business. (28)

In some cases the client will not even know who his lawyer is, that is to say, who is actually doing the work for him. This happens when the referring lawyer does not want the client to know that he has farmed out the matter (e.g., to a "ghost brief writer") because of the risk of losing the client to the other lawyer. As one respondent remarked:

> Usually I'll let my client know I'm referring it, but it's not always wise; you can lose clients that way. (16)

A close, trust relationship is probably rarely achieved in the type of practice to which we have just been referring, not only because of the volume-merchandising phenomenon and the importance of the broker but also because most such matters are handled on a contingency basis that gives the lawyer a direct financial stake in the matter. For this reason the client often becomes, literally, a piece of business.

2. "Clients are partners." Unlike the lawyers discussed above, the upper-level real estate and business-corporate lawyers frequently have a close, intimate relationship with their business clients, so much so in fact that many become merged with their clients on something like a business partnership basis. Well over half go in on deals with clients, principally in the area of real estate, and several are officers or on the board of directors of their clients' corporations. Under these conditions it would appear to be difficult to maintain a fiduciary relationship with the client or to adopt toward him an attitude of disinterestedness. A number of respondents recognize the dangers involved in becoming "partners" of their clients, but, nevertheless, they feel that this is the only way to "make it" financially in the law practice.

> They told us in law school to stick to the law business and it will take care of you—don't go into business with your clients, no deals or arrangements, you lose your perspective, you really become a partner of your client. But this is baloney. If you're invited to go in, go in by all means; it's the only way to get any financial independence —it's the only way to make it. You can't do it practicing law, you can't get any financial security that way. Ninety per cent of the lawyers can't make it—I haven't to date. (6)

NOTES

1. Citations to the Canons in this chapter are made with reference to the Canons of Professional Ethics of the American Bar Association as adopted at the 31st annual meeting of the ABA on August 27, 1908, with later additions and amendments. For an outstanding commentary on the Canons, see Henry S. Drinker, *Legal Ethics* (New York: Columbia Univ. Press, 1953).

2. Prohibitions against solicitation are contained principally in Canons 27 and 28. They read in part as follows:

Canon 27. Advertising, Direct or Indirect

It is unprofessional to solicit professional employment by circulars, advertisements, through touters or by personal communication or interviews not warranted by personal relations. Indirect advertisements for professional employment such as furnishing or inspiring newspaper comments, or procuring his photograph to be published in connection with causes in which the lawyer has been or is engaged or concerning the manner of their conduct, the magnitude of the interest involved, the importance of the lawyer's position, and all other like self-laudation, offend the traditions and lower the tone of our profession and are reprehensible; but the customary use of simple professional cards is not improper [as amended in 1937 and 1940].

Canon 28. Stirring Up Litigation, Directly or Through Agents

It is unprofessional for a lawyer to volunteer advice to bring a law suit. . . . Stirring up strife is not only unprofessional, but it is indictable at common law. It is disreputable to hunt up defects in titles or other causes of action and inform thereof in order to be employed to bring suit or collect judgement, or to breed litigation by seeking out those with claims for personal injuries or those having any other grounds of action in order to secure them as clients, or to employ agents or runners for like purposes, or to pay or reward, directly or indirectly, those who bring or influence the bringing of such cases to his office, or to remunerate policemen, court or prison officials, physicians, hospital *attachés* or others who may succeed, under the guise of giving disinterested friendly advice, in influencing the criminal, the sick and the injured, the ignorant or others, to seek his professional services. A duty to the public and to the profession devolves upon every member of the Bar having knowledge of such practices upon the part of any practitioner immediately to inform thereof, to the end that the offender may be disbarred [as amended in 1928].

3. Karl N. Llewellyn, *Law and Contemporary Problems*, pp. 115–116.

4. George Sharswood, "An Essay on Professional Ethics" (Philadelphia: Reprinted by the ABA in Vol. XXXII of the *Reports of the American Bar Association,* 1907). Interestingly enough, the Alabama Code was somewhat more permissive on the matter of advertising than the present ABA Canons, declaring: "Newspaper advertisements, circulars, and business cards, tendering professional services to the general public are proper," but the Alabama Code went on to add that, "special solicitation to particular individuals to become clients ought to be avoided" (Rule 16, Code of Ethics, Alabama Bar Association, adopted Dec. 14, 1887). Furthermore, George W. Warvelle, in a treatise entitled "Legal Ethics," argued as long ago as 1902 that, although advertising was not necessary in a small town, it was nevertheless needed in the larger cities, "but he opposed any but modest advertisements and severely condemned lawyers advertising their talents 'like shopkeepers' wares'" (George B. Harris, "Ethics of the Legal Profession, 1836–1908," unpublished essay, 1955).

5. See particularly Canons 3 and 32, which read in part as follows:
Canon 3.   Attempts to Exert Personal Influence on the Court
Marked attention and unusual hospitality on the part of a lawyer to a Judge, uncalled for by the personal relations of the parties, subject both the Judge and the lawyer to misconstructions of motive and should be avoided. A lawyer should not communicate or argue privately with the Judge as to the merits of a pending case, and he deserves rebuke and denunciation for any device or attempt to gain from a Judge personal consideration or favor.

Canon 32.   The Lawyer's Duty in Its Last Analysis

No client, corporate or individual, however powerful, nor any cause, civil or political, however important, is entitled to receive nor should any lawyer render any service or advice involving disloyalty to the law whose ministers we are, or disrespect of the judicial office, which we are bound to uphold, or corruption of any person or persons exercising a public office or private trust, or deception or betrayal of the public. When rendering any such improper service or advice, the lawyer invites and merits stern and just condemnation.

6. In Canon 32 "fidelity to private trust" is declared to be one of the principal duties of the lawyer. This requirement of fiduciary self-restraint, of representing the client with "undivided fidelity," includes the obligation not to divulge confidences of a client (neither for the "personal benefit or gain" of the lawyer nor to the disadvantage of the client—see Canons 11 and 37) and the prohibition against representing conflicting interests (see Canon 6). Canon 35, which deals with intermediaries, reads in part:

35.   Intermediaries

The professional services of a lawyer should not be controlled or exploited by any lay agency, personal or corporate, which intervenes between client and lawyer. A lawyer's responsibilities and qualifications are individual. He should avoid all relations which direct the performance of his duties by or in the interest of such intermediary. A lawyer's relation to his client should be personal, and the responsibility should be direct to the client [as amended in 1933].

5

The Anatomy of Dissatisfaction

Finding himself on the lowest rung of the status ladder of the profession, with little or no chance of rising, his practice restricted to the least remunerative and least desirable matters—to the dirty work of the profession, and beset by competition from lawyers and laymen alike, the individual practitioner is frequently a dissatisfied, disappointed, resentful, angry man. Consider, for example, a lawyer whom I shall call Steven.

Steven was born in Chicago in 1920 of Polish immigrant parents. His father, who had no formal education, owned a small grocery store on the Southwest Side. While still in high school Steven decided to become a lawyer. Upon graduation from a night law school he went to work for an insurance company as a claims adjuster. After six months he left that job and went out on his own. Asked what problems he had in getting started, Steven replied:

Getting business. This is a great profession if someone is feeding you business. You can't get business and work at the law at the same time—you can't do both, you'd be on the go 24 hours a day if you'd do that. . . .

Interviewer: Have you solved the problem of getting business?

Respondent: It's still a problem. There's too much competition—cutthroat competition.

Interviewer: What kind of competition?

Respondent: I have a South Side office also. People go shopping, they see you or someone else. They'll come back and say, "The other guy will do it cheaper." There's also competition from real estate brokers, and from savings and loan associations—that cuts something terrific. They draw leases, close real estate deals. Take ——— [a savings and loan association on the Southwest Side]. People go to ——— and I never see them again. They refer them to other lawyers or do the work right there. People come in for a loan, they say, "You don't need a lawyer, we'll do it here."

Interviewer: Any others?

Respondent: Yes, insurance brokers—and accountants also. The difficulty on the South Side is that real estate and insurance brokers get a cut of the fee when they refer cases to certain lawyers—it must be, there's no other reason for it. I know in a few instances where I personally found out about that kind of fee splitting. . . .

Interviewer: What kind of clients do you have?

Respondent: I don't have any rich clients. I have clients it's hard to get money from. . . . Mostly working-class people, three or four small businesses and two or three corporations: a small barrel factory, a small machine shop, an electrical motor sales and service, a small tool-casting corporation, and a used car dealer. . . .

The bulk of his clients, he said, come on recommendations from other clients. Once in a while he gets a referral from another lawyer:

> Mostly in work they didn't want to handle—not enough money in it, and they feel that if the client didn't know the lawyer who was handling it he might get a better fee out of it. . . .
> *Interviewer:* Do you handle any personal injury matters?
> *Respondent:* Very small. That's handled mostly through chasers. Even if a friend's involved they're signed up before you know about it. If I could afford it I'd have a bunch of chasers working for me. I know lawyers who have 'em. They make money.
> *Interviewer:* Have runners ever approached you?
> *Respondent:* Yes, but I haven't done any business with them. They want money for referrals and, secondly, the cases they refer you—you have to advance money, and I'm in no position to advance money. . . .
> *Interviewer:* Any tax foreclosure matters?
> *Respondent:* No; I did. I don't get a lot of it any more. I used to get—I just got out of it. Too much of a headache. That involved pay-offs to individuals—I couldn't stomach it.
> *Interviewer:* Who did you have to pay off?
> *Respondent:* Right along the line, going into any court; if you don't shell out money, you wait.

Asked how important he thought political connections were in the practice of law, he replied that they were all-important, especially in the outcome of cases in the local courts.

> *Interviewer:* But isn't there a remedy through appeal?
> *Respondent:* In the Municipal Court, people in that

court don't have money for an appeal. The attitude of the judges is, if you don't like my ruling, appeal. But in 99 per cent of the cases they're not appealed.

Interviewer: Have you used or developed your own political connections?

Respondent: Yes, in defense I've built up my own political contacts and I've been successful in some instances. I've had matters where the judge was approached from both sides—he was so afraid he referred it to another judge. . . .

Interviewer: In what sense do you believe the practice of law is a profession?

Respondent: That's difficult to give an opinion on. I think it's a glorified rat race.

Interviewer: Because of the competition?

Respondent: Not so much, but the way it's carried on. Take, for instance, personal injury. The big men have the chasers getting business for them. It's difficult to phrase. Attorneys themselves cut prices, they knock another lawyer they don't even know. People have told me that attorneys have been knocking me. Then your big law firms have everything tied up.

Interviewer: Have all the good business, you mean?

Respondent: Yah. The Bar Association could rectify this, but they haven't done it. That's my main reason for not joining the Chicago Bar Association. Of the 15,000 lawyers—the Chicago Bar Association is nonrepresentative, only a small percentage belong. . . . The Chicago Bar Association seems to be a closely knit organization of big firms who don't give a damn about the little guy. I will join the Southwest Bar Association—they recently started a lawsuit against one of the savings and loan associations. The Chicago Bar Association has never done this.

Interviewer: What do you think are the most important differences between lawyers and doctors?

Respondent: First of all, they [doctors] have more respect from laymen and make more money. It seems to me when an individual talks about a lawyer he looks at you like you're a big thief.

Interviewer: What makes for a successful lawyer?

Respondent: Getting the business. If it's coming through the door, you'll be successful.

Interviewer: Who are the most successful lawyers in Chicago?

Respondent: I wouldn't know how to answer that. I'd say from the monetary standpoint, the big law firms.

Interviewer: How successful do you think you have been in the practice of law?

Respondent: Financially, not too well so far.

Interviewer: Have you been satisfied in the practice of law?

Respondent: No.

Interviewer: Would you still be a lawyer if you had it to do all over again?

Respondent: You mean would I do something else? Yes, I'd go into the medical profession. (7)

Although Steven is probably angrier than most, his complaints, his bitterness, his evident dissatisfaction with the practice of law would strike a responsive chord in many of the lawyers interviewed.

Let us consider now the major factors that might account for this general theme of dissatisfaction.

One source of the individual practitioner's dissatisfaction with the practice of law lies in his continuing struggle to make a living in the face of severe competition. Therefore, one would expect the lawyers making the least money and with the most restricted type of practice to be most dissatisfied. That is just what we do find.[1]

More broadly viewed, however, dissatisfaction is not simply an economic problem, for in addition to these difficulties the individual lawyer faces a serious status dilemma that, as we shall see later in this chapter, is generally most severe precisely for those lawyers who have made it financially.

THE STATUS DILEMMA

While mere entry into a profession represents a considerable achievement for most individual practitioners, the fact that they have been unable, for the most part, to rise above the lowest status level of the bar is undoubtedly a major source of their dissatisfaction.

As stated in Chapter 1, most individual practitioners go into the practice of law because of some vague desire for professional status. Their decision to become lawyers rather than some other type of professional man was based principally on the fact that law appeared to provide the easiest and cheapest avenue to professional status. But, largely because of the very route they have taken into the profession (via the night law school with its minimal admission requirements and its barely adequate training), they find that access to the higher status positions is all but closed to them and that the positions they do mange to achieve are often marginal, their practice residual, and their foothold in the profession precarious.

In addition to the restrictions placed on their chances of moving into a more elevated type of practice, most individual practitioners find that they are cut off almost completely from any meaningful professional contact with the higher-status leaders of the bar. Evidence for this last proposition, although not conclusive, is very persuasive:

1. Individual practitioners exchange business primarily with and are on the opposite side in transactions from other individual practitioners or lawyers in the smaller firms. It is conceivable that the upper-level real estate and business-corporate lawyers might be involved in deals in which a large firm lawyer represents the other side; however, only one lawyer in the sample (an upper-level business-corporate lawyer) mentioned specifically that he dealt in this manner with a large firm. The most likely area of work contact would seem to be in the referral of local tax and collections matters from the larger firms. Two local tax specialists (one in the sales tax and the other in the tax foreclosure field) mentioned that a small part of their referrals come from big firms; and the collections specialist mentioned an instance in which he was given an account to collect by a large firm. The only indication of a referral of business outside these areas, and also the only hint of any actual collaboration on such matters, is to be found in the statement of a respondent who is the general counsel of an oil company. "Large firms," he said, "come to me and I advise them on oil matters." (43)

2. Not only do we find little evidence of any effective work contact between individual practitioners and lawyers in the larger firms, but there appears to be virtually no exchange of advice or information on professional matters on an informal basis between the two. In answer to the question, "Whom do you go to when you have a legal problem you can't handle or if you get into difficulty on a case or matter and you want to talk it over with someone?" only three respondents said that they would seek advice from a lawyer in a large firm. In answer to the question, "Do lawyers come to you for advice?" none said that law-

yers from large firms did so—with the exception of the oil company general counsel.

3. Contact with big firm lawyers in the principal professional associations is largely limited by the fact that individual practitioners are far less likely to be members than lawyers in firms,[2] and that only a small proportion of those who are members are active participators. Thus only seven respondents said that they had ever been on a committee of the Illinois State or Chicago Bar Association, and only three said that they had been active members of such committees.

If we consider the two professional organizations that are generally recognized to be the most exclusive and highest status associations of lawyers in Chicago, the Law Club and the Legal Club, we find that while 13 per cent of lawyers in firms of ten or more lawyers are members of one of these clubs, none of the individual lawyers interviewed were members.[3]

The individual practitioner is usually more at home —and is much more likely to be active—in the various ethnic bar associations, such as the Decalogue Society for Jewish lawyers, the Cook County Bar Association for Negro lawyers, the Advocates Society for Polish lawyers, the Catholic Lawyers Guild, the Lutheran Bar Association, and so on. However, in these associations there are practically no lawyers from the larger firms.

Thus it would appear that the bar associations provide little opportunity for meaningful contact between the two extreme segments of the Chicago bar, and, if anything, these associations seem to reinforce the status divisions in the bar.

Given this wide and usually unbridgeable gulf between the two extremes of the bar, it is quite understandable that the individual practitioner will view his colleagues in the wood-paneled suites high up in the towers of the LaSalle Street office buildings with a mixture of awe, resentment, and disbelief—disbelief that he is somehow part of the same profession that includes these exalted individuals who so clearly run the show, but a show that he is privileged only to watch—rarely, if ever, to participate in. As one lawyer remarked in answer to the question of who were the most successful lawyers in Chicago:

> Some of them in the big firms—they have such big offices. The ——— firm, I know some stenographers there. (49)

One way in which the individual practitioner's low status in the bar is most effectively brought home to him is through his virtual exclusion from positions of formal leadership in the bar. Although a little over half the lawyers in Chicago are individual practitioners, less than 20 per cent, for example, of the 95 committee chairmen and vice-chairmen of the Chicago Bar Association in 1956 were individual practitioners, and only 16 per cent of the officers and members of the Board of Managers were individual practitioners. Lawyers from firms with ten or more lawyers, on the other hand, representing only 7 per cent of the lawyers in Chicago, constitute 32 per cent of the committee chairmen and vice-chairmen and 52 per cent of the officers and members of the Board of Managers of the Chicago Bar Association.[4]

The only real chance the individual lawyer has for leadership within professional associations is in the ethnic bar associations; and this, of course, follows from the fact that membership in these associations consists almost wholly of individual practitioners and lawyers in the smallest firms.[5]

That the individual practitioner is often acutely aware of his pariah position in a highly stratified professional community is evidenced in his answers to the question as to whether the major bar associations (especially the Chicago Bar Association) are controlled by any particular group of lawyers. Roughly two out of three respondents gave an affirmative answer to this question, about half identifying the controlling group either as "the larger firms" or in more colorful terms as the "bluenoses," the "snobs," the "upper echelon who don't mix," the "very successful big shots," the "holier-than-thou clique," the "stiffnecks," and so on. A good many of these lawyers expressed considerable bitterness, anger, and resentment in their answers. The language in the following quotations conveys something of their intense feeling on the subject:

> *Interviewer:* How representative are the large bar associations?
> *Respondent:* Very little.
> *Interviewer:* Are they controlled by certain segments of the bar?
> *Respondent:* Yes, I think so. Put it this way, we [the Jewish lawyers] have the Decalogue; the Colored, the Cook County; and the Slavs and the Poles have their associations. The reason for this is that there is something missing in the social life of the Chicago Bar Association. The whole setup is wrong, too many snobs in the higher echelons who don't mix. Seventy per cent of the lawyers have terrific problems and they're confused because there's no leadership to discuss it. These are economic problems. I'm a member of the Chicago Bar Association; I attended, they had special studies, experts would come, we could attend meetings, and specialists would come—it was interesting—on income tax, social security, corporations, all very helpful. But what they can't get into

their heads: a lawyer who has a family, there's sickness, he suffers an economic loss, the high cost of business. Up until last year the leaders of the bar fought social security—his future in old age was of no interest to them—they're in the upper income brackets. They've failed miserably—they're not interested in the masses of lawyers. (26)

There's a clique at the head [of the Chicago Bar Association], the fellows who made their way—holier-than-thou—frowning on activities they engaged in while going up the ladder. There aren't enough lawyers from the ghetto. Too many "well born." No Jimmy Brown, but J. Otis Brown. You get the idea? (4)

They [the Chicago Bar Association] represent the layman against the lawyer, rather than the lawyer's view; instead of protecting the lawyer, they hurt him. And there's class. . . . If a member of a well-known wealthy law firm is brought before the Bar Association for unethical practices, it's not the same decision your poor struggling lawyer will get. . . . The Canons should recognize that the function of the lawyer is not just to serve mankind but to make a livelihood. It shouldn't be one-sided. If a man seeks a wealthy client and invites out some man to get business, takes him on a trip, tips on the stock market—what's the difference between that and solicitation directly? I've felt this way for years. If you're on the grievance committee of the Chicago Bar Association, and you don't handle any of that [personal injury, divorce, etc.] business, O.K. But if you step on *their* toes . . . Why not a big stink by the Bar Association over banks, real estate offices pulling down the dignity of the profession of law? The reason is they can't [implying that the lawyers in the large firms are directors of the banks, etc.]. The dignity of the law—they set up standards so high no one can follow. But if they come down, they then would help the lawyer, push the lawyer. (88)

The bar is controlled, but there have been some inroads so that the bluenoses alone won't be completely in—but they still control the association. The great percentage of the members don't take too much interest. I definitely feel, from a political standpoint, [there is] control of the Chicago Bar Association, control of the management in the main, from the policy set forth and its opinions about other lawyers. I'm also opposed to the Judicial Reform Bill, if you'd like to hear about that. [As he went on to discuss this matter he became more and more agitated, so that at the end he could hardly contain himself.] It's a misrepresentation, like the Americans for Democratic Action (it can be the most undemocratic, controlled by Communists, etc.), or the D.A.R. This Judicial Reform would in effect put a few firms in charge of every judge. The small practitioner wouldn't have a chance in hell. . . . A man like [Judge] Harry Fisher, they [the Chicago Bar Association] wouldn't put their stamp on, they call him unqualified one minute and ten minutes later they call him qualified. Some of the big firms got mad at his decisions—the big insurance companies almost railroaded him. The big firms, insurance companies, they have all the money, the newspapers—and they can deceive outsiders with talk of Judicial Reform. . . . The Board of Managers [of the Chicago Bar Association] will then control the whole judiciary. A client will have to go into the big law firms. And the individual lawyer, with all the merits in a case can't win if the firm wants it the other way—the judge won't jeopardize 200 [large-firm] votes. [Prior to giving its recommendations on candidates in the Judicial election, the Chicago Bar Association polls its membership as to the qualifications of candidates. While not an explicit provision in any of the Judicial Reform bills, it was believed by many lawyers that if the Reform bill were passed judges would be selected from a list drawn up by a nominating commission of the Chicago Bar Association, and that this commission would consist mainly of lawyers in the larger firms. This respondent, however, seemed to believe that judges would be selected on the basis of a membership poll of the Chicago Bar Association in which the large firms would vote as a block.] Leaving it to the ward committeeman, that's bad too, but at least you have some recourse if it gets too bad. If I have to choose between the ward committeeman and the Bar Association—those bluenoses! Let's not give the bunch— the small group who control the big firms—the control of the judiciary! That's the basis of our whole system, the jury trial! . . . The insurance companies are trying to wipe out the juries! It's one thing to fix one judge, but twelve jurors. The jury system is our best—jurors aren't so dumb, they do O.K. percentage-wise. (33)

I don't like the Chicago Bar Association. We [personal injury lawyers] feel they're dominated by a small group of blue-blood lawyers. Their interests are not compatible with ours. They are the lawyers that represent the railroads and insurance companies. (36)

The fact is it [the Chicago Bar Association] is run by the big firms with forty to fifty votes—it's run for the benefit of the insurance companies, the railroads and the big corporations. (27)

Interviewer: Is the bar association representative of the average lawyer?
Respondent: I'd say no. It's representative of a—well that's the reason why you have the Hellenic, the Justinian, the Jew, Polack associations.
Interviewer: You feel it's controlled by the large firms?
Respondent: Hell, yes. If not, then why do the Polish lawyers have their association, and so on . . . [Later, at the close of the interview, the respondent pointed out apropos of the disciplinary function of the Chicago Bar

Association:] A big thief never gets caught, but a little guy takes $500 of his client's money and he gets the book thrown at him. (37)

Several lawyers, in speaking of the Chicago Bar Association, commented on the endorsement "fiasco" of Judge Harry Fisher, which was cited as a prime example of the controlling voice of the large firms in setting the policies of the association. (The Chicago Bar Association at first did not endorse Judge Fisher as candidate in the judicial election, then later reversed itself.) In the view of these respondents, Judge Fisher was a man who meted out justice, a friend of the little guy, but who had made enemies of some big firm lawyers and was being treated rather shabbily because of it.

Those respondents who were most resentful about the dominance of the large firms in the bar association are the more successful lawyers, particularly those in the local tax, divorce, and personal injury areas. The practice of these lawyers, as pointed out earlier, is confined to matters that the large firms generally will not handle, not so much because they are unremunerative—some of the lawyers specializing in these areas (not necessarily those in our sample) have the largest incomes of any lawyers in private practice—but because they bear the taint of graft and corruption. These matters are the dirty work of the profession, and the lawyers who handle them, although widely known, are generally regarded as engaging in questionable practices of an unethical nature and are frequently labeled as ambulance chasers, tax fixers, operators of divorce mills, and so on. As a consequence of the notorious character of their practice, and of the patently unethical arrangements in which a good many of them are involved, personal injury, tax, and divorce lawyers become the favorite targets of the bar association's periodic campaigns to "get" the chasers and the fixers. It is quite understandable, therefore, that these lawyers, especially those who have been most successful financially, would feel the pinch of the status structure most keenly and, hence, would feel most resentful about the restrictions placed on their chances for further mobility and higher status.

The upper-level real estate and business-corporate lawyers are generally less sensitive to large firm control than the lawyers just discussed. This probably results from the fact that being closer to the large firm lawyers in terms of their clientele and the type of work in which they engage, they are more likely to find compensations for whatever restrictions in status they experience. These lawyers have not only the advantage of a more permanent business clientele and a greater sense of accomplishment in their work, but they have also been able to carve out a fairly secure niche for themselves in the practice of law. Although they may feel restricted to a limited range of matters, several asserted quite confidently that within that range they could do as good a job (if not a better one) as the lawyers in the large firms. Note in this regard the remarks of an upper-level business-corporate lawyer on the question of the relative merits of the individual practitioner versus the big firm in servicing corporate clients:

> The average client, if he's not too large, is far better off with a small law firm than a big one. There aren't too many competitive features from the big firm. For example, in a small firm, if you get an enormous problem requiring the work of a great many lawyers, a small firm can't engage those people, while the large firm has a staff at its disposal, therefore [on such matters] you can't really compete. But

a large firm having a large overhead and a staff—that makes for a greater charge for matters of nominal importance than a small firm. . . . There is an upward limit of the size of corporation I can handle, but in a specific situation it might not be so. I'm qualified to take on any problem, but in the antitrust field, litigations, I don't have the immediate facilities for examining documents, thousands of pieces of paper, to get issues in form, details.

Interviewer: Are you at a disadvantage in not being able to give a wide range of advice?

Respondent: Yes, but the large firm has the disadvantage of anonymity. That's a disturbing factor for many clients— there are people who came to me from large firms because of that—they didn't know whom they were going to deal with. (68)

Another upper-level business-corporate lawyer was far more aggressive in comparing the relative merits of the individual practitioner and the big firm:

The big difference between the large firm lawyer and the average practitioner is that the big firms give out more bullshit, superfluity, and unnecessary research. They look for too many technicalities—they can charge for every second of time. The smaller client, however, is aware of the costs of retaining counsel. The lawyer ought to cut down on the time he spends on unnecessary work. The error is to be too legalistic. Clients want results. (50)

The less successful lower-level lawyers, finding themselves furthest removed from the center of things in the practice—at the very margin of the bar, with not even a hope of breaking into the elite—are quite naturally least disturbed by large firm control. Being most involved in the scramble to make a living, their chief concern is still economic. The few who were disturbed about large firm control of the Chicago Bar Association were not so much registering a complaint against the closed structure of the bar as expressing their resentment about the intense economic problems they face, and their bitterness toward the leaders of the bar for not doing anything about it, for having forgotten about them. In their view the bar associations have failed to protect the small practitioner from the encroachment of nonlawyers, have done nothing about improving his economic position, and apply a more stringent standard in judging his conduct than in judging the conduct of lawyers in the larger firms. In speaking of the hostility of the bar association toward the individual practitioner, one lawyer pointed out:

> Here the bar association belittles you. The bar association is used as a club over the lawyer. In Europe they protect the lawyer. One lawyer wouldn't talk against another lawyer. But we need policing, I suppose. (84)

THE ILLUSION OF INDEPENDENCE

With very few exceptions the individual practitioner places a high value on being his own boss. A lower-level personal injury lawyer, when asked what advice he would give a young man just starting out, replied without hesitation:

> I say be independent, on your own. What's the purpose of being a lawyer if you work for someone else? You might

as well go into business. [He paused for a moment, then added:] Of course then you'd make more money, and probably feel happier. (88)

This lawyer had many second thoughts on the practice of law, but about one thing he was certain: If you practice law, be independent. At another point in the interview he commented:

> One fine feature of being a lawyer, his time is his own, he doesn't have to be down at a certain time or leave at a certain time.

This theme of being your own boss, of not having to account to anyone, was repeated over and over again by lawyers in all levels and areas of practice:

> "I like being by myself, I prefer to be by myself, I don't like to be bossed."
>
> "If he's imaginative, has courage, a person should be by himself."
>
> "I'm an independent individual, I always felt I could get by on my own efforts."
>
> "I'd advise any young man with any confidence in himself, with any personality, to take a job by himself instead of taking a job with someone."
>
> "If he has guts, perseverance, and is unafraid, he should go out on his own."
>
> "Self-mastery is the most important single matter—he should be his own boss."
>
> "I'm by myself, always have been; I like it, get my kicks from doing it myself."
>
> "I don't want to be tied down to other people, I don't have to account to others about my time; I do what I please and when I please."
>
> "You're your own boss, that appeals to me."

Several claimed that they could make more money in business or that they might be better off working for someone else, or in a firm, but they felt it was more important to be on their own.

> Sometimes I thought I'd be better off financially in the business world. But there are compensations—you're your own employer—your own time. (80)

> The boys in firms make more money, they're better organized than the individual practitioner, but it's not as rich an experience. (67)

> Statistics show that those in partnerships make more money. This may be, but I rather like it the way I am. Didn't Caesar say he'd rather be first in a little Tiberian village than second in Rome? (34)

> I'd be better off working for someone else, but I can't—I'm not temperamentally suited for it. (6)

Closely related to the theme of independence, is the feeling that the individual practitioner is the real lawyer, or more of a real lawyer than his colleagues in the large firms.

> I had occasion to deal with a senior member of a firm who spends more in purchasing office supplies than I make in four years. He didn't know what a guarantee of an easement was; he didn't recognize the essential requirement in that basis, because without that guarantee you're land-locked with fifty acres. (37)

> I know lawyers in big firms who couldn't try a case. (88)

> I know lawyers who make in excess of $60,000 and they don't even know what a complaint looks like. (6)

I'm a general attorney, I do everything myself. I'm a big-town small-time country attorney. I handle it from the time it comes in—I may not try a case, but I don't delegate any of my functions. (44)

I know a lot of lawyers—to me unsuccessful. They have amassed large bank accounts but never have been to the Supreme Court of Illinois, nothing to do with making the law of our state. How can you call them successful law-yers? (55)

These lawyers, although generally handling matters that require little in the way of technical legal skill, still have fairly frequent contact with the courts and are thereby able to find a link with the most commonly accepted image of the lawyer. In contrast to the individual practitioner, the big firm lawyer, in their view, has not only lost his identity as a real lawyer by virtue of his more infrequent contact with the courts ("they couldn't try a case" and "don't even know what a complaint looks like") but his independence as well:

A young lawyer if he's looking for experience, he's grad-uated law school, he's better off in a small firm or with an individual practitioner for experience—more responsibili-ties, he'll learn more practical routine, the procedures. If he goes to work for a big firm he'll become a cog in a tre-mendous machine, assigned to a particular phase and learn it, but no experience in multiplicity, which he needs if he goes into general practice. You only learn by doing, and you're only in one field in a big firm. Barring connections in the firm, no matter how attractive the offer, you get buried away, and after a few years you become a slave to that firm. (33)

I wouldn't advise a complete extrovert to go into a well-established firm—the stodginess, and too protected. (47)

> *Interviewer:* Would you advise someone to go into a large firm?
>
> *Respondent:* Not unless he has independent connections, otherwise he would get buried. (36)

The strongest expression of confidence in the ethos of independence is the overwhelmingly large proportion (over 75 per cent) from all levels and areas of practice who advise a prospective lawyer either initially or eventually to go into practice on his own. Only those who are most extremely dissatisfied with the practice of law would not recommend that he go out on his own and only a handful suggest ending up in a corporate legal department or in a large firm.

Tied in with the notion of being the real lawyers is the conviction voiced by a sizable proportion of respondents that there is no positive correlation between financial success and ability, that the best lawyers can't make any money.

> The best lawyer I knew was my uncle, but he never made a living from it. He loved it, and was acquainted with its workings.
>
> *Interviewer:* How successful do you think you have been in the practice of law?
>
> *Respondent:* From a money point of view, no. If you're asking, am I a competent lawyer, the answer is yes. I make a bare living from the law. (6)

> I know many successful ones who never made a great deal of money. (82)

> What makes a successful lawyer? A wealthy family. Connections. You can be the most astute lawyer; but if there is nothing to exercise your astuteness on, you can politely flush it down the drain. You can be the most stupid horse's

ass on two feet, but if you're the son of Mr. So-and-so you're a successful lawyer without having the slightest conception of a real legal doctrine. (37)

I know a lot of successful lawyers dollar-wise, but few who gained eminence because [they were] good lawyers for clients. (65)

I know many failures who are able; they can't win the confidence of a client. (22)

I always say a lawyer doesn't have to know too much law to be successful, he just has to have a good clientele. If he has, he can hire people with ability. It's not what you know but who you know. (86)

When you say success—such a relative term—one might consider it from a material point of view, others from the ethical point of accomplishment or service, another from the honor point of view, not for material gain but honor bestowed on them in services rendered.
Interviewer: What is your definition?
Respondent: Mine is a cross section of these points of view. Quite a few are starving as ethical lawyers—and are happy. Others amass money in six or seven figures. (75)

Some lawyers judge [success] by money, others ability, others prestige.
Interviewer: And yourself?
Respondent: Frankly, without some monetary consideration [you're] not [a] successful attorney. To myself—ability —I know many able attorneys who are not successful financially, not earning a living even. The correlation between ability and ability to earn is small. It's larger in the medical profession. (63)

The argument that there is a lack of correspondence between ability and success becomes complicated by the underlying recognition on the part of many respondents of the modest degree of their own legal ability. This frequently results, on the one hand, in a curious combination of respect for ability and indignation over the fact that it doesn't count for as much as it should and, on the other, contempt for ability and those who possess it—you can always buy ability. This view provides the individual lawyer with a convenient explanation or rationalization not only of his lack of success (because ability is not rewarded) but also of his relatively low level of technical skill (since at best legal ability is a cheap and not very valuable commodity and therefore it is no great loss not to have it).

Although the individual practitioner may argue quite seriously that he is independent, he himself is only too well aware of the illusory nature of such a position, of the harsh realities of individual practice that make such a position well-nigh untenable. The hardest reality to escape from is the economic problem. Caught in the economic squeeze, the individual practitioner is highly dubious of the possibilities of making it as an individual practitioner, at least without some outside financial interests. Independence then becomes either an empty or an illusory concept.

Well over half the lawyers maintained that the individual practitioner has little chance of success in the practice of law.[6] Many were quite bitter about it:

> You ought to make up your mind right now, successful lawyers are successful because of outside activities, real estate, in the market, or stocks of the clients—and when they have money, they're asked to put it up—they get into syndicates. . . . I feel sorry for lawyers I meet, they're having a terrible time—they can't dress properly—you have to have a high standard of living. Only thing to do is to get out. How many have been forced to go into other fields.

The truth of it is, if I knew another business I'd throw it up for grabs—although I've liked the work. Other lawyers more and more can't take it—the guff when clients come in and call at all hours of the day and night, criticize and insult you to get results. You don't have to take that. Those who have specialized and have done well, in the divorce angle, etc., they can be independent—clients do things their way or else. (26)

Several respondents insisted that having outside financial interests was the only way to achieve any economic independence. One lawyer, although he felt it was improper to go in on deals with clients, conceded:

But you can't make any money from the practice of law. If you want your kids to live in a decent neighborhood, take a vacation—it takes money. (16)

Even the most successful lawyers in the sample, in terms of income and clientele, were highly skeptical of the opportunities for success in individual practice. An elderly upper-level business-corporate lawyer whose father had been an individual practitioner before him remarked:

I have two sons just going into the practice. I told them both that I think the day of the individual practitioner is over in this city. I think they should try to practice in a firm, in a large firm. The business is being concentrated. These large firms are the department stores of the law business. If a fellow has something, he can get in and show it— he would find himself a niche. By himself he'll be starving, he won't get any substantial clients. He'll get his friends, from his own contacts—gradually build up something. And so many fields no longer exist: no lawyer now is a financial adviser, advises on mortgages, examines titles, becomes a trustee—it's all gone into the corporations. Take your big

> commercial concerns, they all have big law firms that can furnish any legal service they need. ——— [a large firm in Chicago] has offices in Washington and New York—not a field they can't supply an expert in: income tax, probate— here's your man. (39)

Added to the more general economic problem, and in part growing out of it, is the pattern of dependence-involvement with the business brokers, the ethically questionable arrangements and tactics for getting business and handling matters, the favors, gifts, fee splitting—the emphasis, in short, on business-getting and institutional manipulative skills. All these factors contribute to viewing the practice of law as a business and not a profession, to the conviction that everything depends on connections and favors, and to the feeling of being looked down upon, of enjoying little regard or prestige from the lay public, of being parasites—in short, of not being real lawyers at all.

Close to half the respondents were unable to say without hesitation that the practice of law is a profession [7] and a little over a fourth, including practically all the lawyers in the personal injury field, were clearly convinced that it is not. Note the following answers to the question: "In what sense is the practice of law a profession?"

> To me, I don't think it's a profession. [It's] the same as selling shoestrings. The ethics of the big and small can't be scrutinized too carefully. . . . You can't trust [lawyers]. They'll commingle clients' funds, they'll settle cases without the other lawyer's consent, they'll settle cases for less than they'll admit to clients, or take more than what's necessary to settle. . . . It's too bad the general practice doesn't adhere more closely to the Canons. It's because of the competition in the profession. They must do unscrupulous acts. (12)

In theory only—that's my personal belief. Law is a business based purely on an economic standard. It has moved away from a profession to a business.

Interviewer: What do you mean?

Respondent: It is in theory because the members of the profession are supposed to be restrained by a matter of ethics, which serves as a restraining influence on them. In practice those rules of ethics have been broadened, having as a basic outlook pecuniary gain and getting business.

Interviewer: Is that a bad thing?

Respondent: A necessary, existing evil—it's bad for the law profession. It is this that has reduced the law profession to a business. But it's necessary, without it you couldn't exist. (82)

It's a business to me. The only people that think it is [a profession] are not lawyers.

Interviewer: Do you consider yourself a lawyer or a businessman?

Respondent: Both, very few are not. The only lawyers are those who are hired as pure talent. There's one in this office, he doesn't care about money, he only wants to read the literature and practice law. (27)

The legal profession is, from an economic standpoint, oversupplied to a point where it has degenerated—so it's a question whether it's actually a profession. . . . The only time I have a sense of operating professionally is on the occasions when I talk to people about their estates, on a domestic relations problem—where there's an opportunity to discuss matters. I've had that on a couple of occasions, where people come in ostensibly on legal problems, but other things are involved. (18)

It is [a profession]. It should be, the way it should be practiced, but the way a lot of them do it it's not. I'd like to see it [here] the way it's practiced, the way it is in England, the barristers, they *know* about the cases they handle. But here the lawyer is more like an agent, a middleman.

Interviewer: What do you mean?

Respondent: A lot of the work, in the personal injury field—a good many attorneys procure the business and turn it over to someone else. You know what I mean, you read about it in the newspapers. . . . In every field I presume there are some who get the business and then turn it over to certain other lawyers.

Interviewer: Is there a clear distinction between the practice of law and business?

Respondent: Some of the lawyers are more businessmen than lawyers. (44)

Interviewer: In what sense is the practice of law a profession?

Respondent: Only in the sense that it's classified as such. It's a task. As far as I'm concerned, a doctor is a mechanic.

Interviewer: Is there a clear distinction between the practice of law and a business?

Respondent: No, it's not clear. This law is a business, as far as I'm concerned—to my clients, it's a profession. . . . I'm a lawyer engaged in business. (32)

It's not a profession. I think it's the means of earning a livelihood . . . it's a business, like anything else. Some people like it because it's white collar—you don't have any inventories, but it's a business. The boys I'm with have incomes in six figures, but they don't know any law. . . . It's contacts and getting business, and being able to convince the clients that you're the best. (35)

More than half the respondents were also convinced of the efficacy of political connections in both getting and handling business. Such notions obviously tend to reinforce the widespread belief that in the practice of law it is more "who you know than what you know," that it's all politics and connections.

Painfully aware of the commercial and political character of his practice, the individual practitioner finds it difficult to sustain the claim of independence and of being a real lawyer. Moreover, as these defenses fall away, he is frequently unable to prevent his feelings of insignificance about his job and himself from flooding to the surface. This is very clearly brought out in the answers to the question: "What are the most important differences between lawyers and doctors?"

> Clients. They think a doctor is doing something for them. A lawyer—they try to underestimate your services. They think you charge too much or that there's skulduggery—they think you're going to rob them. While doctors —and they're just as mercenary, if not more—hold themselves above that. He'll have his girl send the bill—while you have to argue with the client about it in the office. Doctors won't talk about fees. A doctor may not operate himself—but they'll say all you [a lawyer] did was make a phone call and put something on paper. There are dedicated doctors and lawyers, but some are out for the dollar —circumstances make it so, they might not want to be. The fellow out in practice is guided by the profit motive like anyone else. In the big firms it's the boys who bring in the business, they don't have to do anything else.

Many respondents felt that while doctors were concerned with matters of life and health, lawyers only deal with clients' financial problems.

> They have lives and the health of patients at stake; in my field there's only money at stake—that's a big difference. (36)

To me a doctor is tops. He does more for humanity than lawyers. We pretty much fool with their pocketbooks. (34)

Doctors are more creative, more abreast of the times. . . . They're filled more with scientific inquiry, there's a curiosity that compels most doctors. . . . Frankly, I take a dim view of most lawyers following a calling having a great impact on our social order. A doctor, engineer, sociologist—the sum total advances the interest of society more than lawyers. The connection with the administration of justice is labored. A doctor, engineer, teacher (I would go into teaching if I had it to do over again), what they are doing, the sum total effect—there is a more direct connection, for example, with some labor lawyers. They make a definite contribution, but for most lawyers I take a dim view of the aggregate effect. What they've contributed to the well-being of their fellow-men I am at a loss to say what it might be. (3)

Well, in so far as rendering a benefit to mankind, a doctor's is a higher profession. His services, figuring out that—looking at it from the standpoint of what does a man need, health is way ahead of property. (39)

I bow to the medical profession. They provide a far greater service to mankind. I put such a great value on health rather than on people's personal problems. To be able to see and hear is more important than solving a wife's problems. (38)

Doctors not only are felt to be engaged in an intrinsically more significant activity, but it is frequently said that they are more respected and enjoy greater prestige in the eyes of the public:

Doctors make a lot more money. The medical profession is more respected in the eyes of the public than lawyers. (2)

They should respect you as a professional man, not as a businessman; there should be some dignity. I always maintained this: in a small town there is more respect for doctors and lawyers, they're known. In the big city a few give the rest a black eye. You read in the papers, the investigations, lawyers involved. To the public a lawyer is nothing but a crook. The masses are scared of a lawyer; they have more respect for a doctor. They are afraid a lawyer will double-cross them. (12)

Moreover, several respondents felt that doctors operate on a higher plane, that they are more dedicated, and more prone to treat one another as colleagues:

Fundamentally there is not a great deal of difference as far as the conduct of practice is concerned. Both are in it for one thing, to make a living, although doctors are a little more dedicated, more conscientious, more thought for the benefit of humanity than the average lawyer. (47)

Doctors make more money. Doctors as between themselves operate on a higher plane for their own society than lawyers do. Doctors won't belittle another doctor, or show him to be wrong as between patient and doctor. But a lawyer won't hesitate to file a complaint against another lawyer. It's more dog eat dog in our profession. (84)

It's not like in medicine, older lawyers don't help out the younger ones, they take advantage of a young fellow. When they're on the other side in court or in negotiation, they try to trip him up by trickery and so on. That's not right—they're all out to make the most they can, they're all out for themselves. (45)

Well, doctors have a damn good union and lawyers don't.
Interviewer: What do you mean?

Respondent: Lawyers have no real—they don't have a professional society of the same figure and power as doctors. A doctor will never testify against another doctor, a lawyer will. (67)

The image of the doctor as possessing all those qualities and attributes that are somehow denied to the lawyer is, as we have seen, often colored by a sense of resentment and envy. Doctors are frequently accused of exploiting patients and of adopting a commercial attitude in their relationship to patients. These accusations are reminiscent of similar charges made by many respondents against their own colleagues; in fact, the doctor is generally damned for being even more extreme in these matters than lawyers:

Doctors exploit people today. I see people pay $800, $900. Lawyers don't get that. They're getting away with murder. There was this doctor from Germany, when he came here he was very poor, had nothing, now he's got two or three six-flat buildings. I took my wife to be examined—$10, $15. You get a prescription, 60 pills cost $11.20, supposed to take four a day. That's a reasonable price? . . . Things like that. My boy got a rupture—$21. They make money but they put on a face. Lawyers got to produce. A doctor always gets $10 a visit. People talk to me half a day and I don't get a nickel. (49)

[Doctors] are more unethical than lawyers. (20)

Doctors are more money-hungry—but they will argue it the other way. (42)

Doctors are making more money. Doctors of today are getting to be a very arrogant class of citizens, getting to a point where it's almost dictatorial. They write the rules and they're pretty tough. There are a lot of very fine ones, the new ones are on the rough side—won't make calls, fees out of line with the services they render. (57)

> When a doctor charges a fee you're happy to pay it, when a lawyer does it's too much. It's easier to practice medicine. If they never went to a doctor 75 per cent would get better, but a doctor gets credit for giving pills—and the Indians didn't all die, did they? or the Christian Scientists? (74)

One personal injury lawyer said that the most important difference between doctors and lawyers is the fact that the former, unlike the latter, are not bound by ethics:

> Doctors are richer. But the main difference is that doctors are not bound so strictly by rules and ethics of the profession as is a lawyer. . . . The doctor only has to work for the client, he doesn't have to worry about other doctors or that a court is telling him he's doing a wrong thing. (82)

Although the notion that doctors have fewer restrictions placed upon them than lawyers may seem a bit odd, especially coming from a personal injury lawyer who previously had complained of the "broadening" of ethical standards in the legal profession to the point where "pecuniary gain" and "getting business" were the basic considerations, the following remarks of a local tax lawyer appear to be an even clearer case of projection:

> Doctors don't know what they're doing—we at least have some basis on which to operate. As you can see, I don't like doctors. My brother-in-law is a doctor, and also my good friend—they at least are honest enough to admit that they're just trying. You give the patient penicillin, and if he survives, all well and good. But by and large doctors do more harm than good. And then no doctor does things

unselfishly. Lawyers, on the other hand, contribute time and money to numerous enterprises. The doctors have had it too good the last few years. (6)

It must be kept in mind, however, that individual lawyers come in contact with a certain level of the medical profession, especially in the personal injury field, under circumstances that might very well lead them to the view that doctors are no more ethical or no less dishonest than many lawyers. A young lawyer just getting started in the personal injury field observed:

> Doctors consider themselves the almighty of mankind, no one has problems but them. The reputation of lawyers with the public is that we are snakes, dishonest, but there are no crooked lawyers without crooked doctors—especially in this field. (25)

To summarize, it has been suggested that the value that most individual practitioners place on being their own boss, combined with the conviction that they, unlike their colleagues in the big firms, are the real lawyers, may be viewed as an attempted inversion of the status hierarchy of the metropolitan bar, a device, in effect, for denying their patently low status. The inadequacy of this device as a solution of the status dilemma has been indicated. We have seen, in fact, that the very opposite feelings—that they have little independence, and that they are not lawyers, or at least not the real lawyers they claim to be—colored by a deep sense of insignificance are equally in evidence in the remarks of the very same respondents. In short, then, *most* individual practitioners in the metropolitan bar are men of fairly high ambition who haven't made it, and try as they may, they cannot rationalize this fact away.

NOTES

1.

TABLE 28

Type of Practice	Per Cent Dissatisfied *	Number of Cases
Lower-Level:		
Real Estate, Business-Corporate	86	(14)
Personal Injury, etc., General Practice	47	(17)
Upper-Level:		
Personal Injury, Tax, Divorce, etc.	44	(17)
Real Estate, Business-Corporate	28	(19)

* Dissatisfaction is defined as a negative response to at least two of the following three questions: How successful do you think you have been in the practice of law? Would you still be a lawyer if you had it to do all over again? Have you been satisfied in the practice of law?

TABLE 29

Income from Practice of Law	Per Cent Dissatisfied	Number of Cases *
Up to $7,500	70	(17)
$7,501–12,000	65	(14)
$12,001–16,500	40	(10)
$16,501–42,000	25	(16)

* No information on income from 10 respondents.

2.

TABLE 30

BAR ASSOCIATION MEMBERSHIP OF CHICAGO LAWYERS,
BY STATUS IN PRACTICE, 1956

(PER CENT OF LAWYERS WHO BELONG)

Bar Association	Individual Practitioners Level of Practice		Lawyers in Firms Size of Firm		
	Lower	Upper	2–9	10–25	26+
American	13	28	30	63	64
Illinois State	32	42	37	50	50
Chicago	36	53	54	75	68
Number of lawyers	(31)	(36)	(92)	(74)	(383)

SOURCE: Figures for individual practitioners based on sample in this study; for lawyers in firms of 2 to 9 lawyers, a random sample drawn from *Sullivan's Law Directory for the State of Illinois* (Chicago: Sullivan's Law Directory, 1956) and checked against *Martindale*, 1956, for law school attended; for lawyers in firms of 10 to 25 lawyers, a random sample from *Martindale*, 1956, biographical section; for lawyers in firms of 26 and more lawyers, all lawyers listed in biographical section of *Martindale*, 1956.

3. Statistics on membership in the Law Club and Legal Club for lawyers in firms of 10 or more lawyers are based on information in biographical section of *Martindale* (see source note to Table 13). While it is conceivable that at least some members of these clubs would appear in a larger sample of individual practitioners, it is most unlikely that more than 1 or 2% of the total population of individual lawyers in Chicago are members.

4.

TABLE 31

PER CENT OF CHICAGO LAWYERS HOLDING OFFICIAL POSITIONS
IN THE CHICAGO BAR ASSOCIATION, BY STATUS IN PRACTICE, 1956

Status in Practice	Officers and Members of Board of Managers (1955–1957)	Committee Chairmen and Vice-Chairmen (1956)	Per Cent of all Chicago Lawyers (1956)
Individual practitioners	16%	19%	54%
Lawyers in firms of 2 to 9	37	31	23
Lawyers in firms of 10 plus	44	40	7
Not in private practice	3	10	16
Total	100%	100%	100%
Number of lawyers	(63)	(95)	(12,000)

SOURCE: Chicago Bar Association, *Annual Reports Submitted by Committees* in the Association (1955–1956, 1956–1957, 1957–1958). Figures for total Chicago lawyers, from same sources as in Table 30.

That the metropolitan individual practitioner is similarly cut off from leadership positions in the American Bar Association is suggested in the following table:

TABLE 32

DISTRIBUTION OF ABA DELEGATES AND TOTAL LAWYERS FOR CITIES OF
500,000 OR MORE, BY STATUS IN PRACTICE, 1955

Status in Practice	Members House of Delegates, ABA	Total Lawyers
Individual Practitioners	17%	58%
Lawyers in firms of 2 to 9	35	17
Lawyers in firms of 10 plus	33	9
Not in private practice	15	16
Total	100%	100%
Number of lawyers	(79)	(83,200)

SOURCE: Names of members drawn from *American Bar Association Directory, 1955–1956* and then checked for status in practice, in *Martindale,* 1956. Distribution of total lawyers in cities of a half million or more compiled from *Lawyers in the United States: Distribution and Income,* Part One: Distribution (Chicago: American Bar Foundation, 1956), Table 14, for 1955 statistics.

5.

TABLE 33

DISTRIBUTION OF CURRENT OFFICERS AND MEMBERS OF THE BOARD OF MANAGERS, AND PAST PRESIDENTS STILL IN PRACTICE OF THE DECALOGUE SOCIETY OF LAWYERS, BY STATUS IN PRACTICE, 1956

Status in Practice	Per Cent
Individual practitioners	69
Lawyers in firms of 2 to 10	22
Not in private practice	9
Total	100
Number of lawyers	(45)

SOURCE: *Sullivan's Law Directory,* 1956–1957.

6.

TABLE 34

Possibilities of "Making It" as an Individual Practitioner	Per Cent
Can't make it ; too tough; stay out	52
Have to have outside financial interests	11
If work hard, get some breaks	37
Total	100
Number of cases	(66)*

* No data from one respondent.

7.

TABLE 35

Is the Practice of Law a Profession?	Per Cent
Definitely is	54
Some don't treat it that way, but it is; not sure	20
Not a profession, but a business; most don't treat it as a profession	26
Total	100
Number of cases	(65) *

* No data from two respondents.

Conclusion

One fact stands out clearly from this study of Chicago lawyers: the lawyer practicing by himself is generally at the bottom of the status ladder of the metropolitan bar. Although once held in the highest esteem as the model of a free, independent professional, today the individual practitioner of law, like the general practitioner in medicine, is most likely to be found at the margin of his profession, enjoying little freedom in choice of clients, type of work, or conditions of practice. While obviously disturbing to the individual lawyer himself, this state of affairs should also be cause for serious concern to the profession as a whole, and especially to the leadership of the bar, in view of the question it raises of the individual practitioner's ability either to practice law in the traditional sense or to live up to the ethical norms of the profession.

In considering the work of the individual lawyer in

Chicago, one is drawn to the conclusion that he is rarely called upon to exercise a high level of professional skill. This arises in part from the generally low quality of his professional training, but even more from the character of the demands placed upon him by the kinds of work and clients he is likely to encounter. Most matters that reach the individual practitioner—the small residential closing, the simple uncontested divorce, drawing up a will or probating a small estate, routine filings for a small business, negotiating a personal injury claim, or collecting on a debt —do not require very much technical knowledge, and what technical problems there are are generally simplified by the use of standardized forms and procedures. Even in those areas where there is presumably greater opportunity for the exercise of legal ingenuity and skill, in handling the more involved real estate and business-corporate matters, the small or even medium-sized businessman is either not interested in or unwilling to pay for the kind of legal advice or product that would give fullest rein to the individual practitioner's abilities. As a result, the legal work of the individual lawyer is, in most instances, reduced to a fairly routine, clerical-bookkeeping job—the very kind of job which many nonlawyers and lay organizations are as well, if not better, equipped to handle than the lawyer. The considerable success that such lay groups have had in taking away this type of business from the lawyer has led to some bitter controversies. The language used by the organized bar in pressing its claims against these lay groups, however, leads one to believe that it is more concerned with preserving its monopoly than with trying to determine how best to serve the public. My own feeling is that much of this work should probably be handled by lay organizations. This does not necessarily mean eliminating the lawyer, but, as in the case of the title company, transferring the job from the private lawyer to the house counsel. Taking over the job of title searching by the title companies, by the way, seems to me a good example of how this shift can be accomplished without detriment to either the legal profession or the public. In any event, this problem deserves a more sober and informed debate by the bar and other interested groups than it apparently has heretofore received.

Another reason why the individual lawyer is only rarely called upon to practice law in the traditional sense is that much of his time is taken up with brokerage activities, serving as middleman between client and other lawyers. Playing the part of broker is to a certain extent, of course, both inevitable and desirable in any profession. Who is in a better position than the lawyer himself to direct clients to the proper colleague on a particular matter? Among individual lawyers, however, it is the economic rather than the professional interest that seems to be at issue in such transactions; the guiding consideration is not who is best trained or most experienced to do the most competent job for the client but who is most likely to get the largest recovery and hence pay the largest commission. While referrals may often become an important and occasionally a very lucrative source of income for the individual practitioner, so far as the client is concerned they constitute an additional expense for which he must ultimately pay. Whether this brokerage system represents a reasonable or desirable mechanism in the marketing of legal services seems to be highly debatable. This is quite obviously another area to which the bar should direct its attention.

Finally, we find a relatively low order of professional skill exercised by individual lawyers because, at this level of practice, more than at any other, results are obtained for clients less on the basis of manipulating legal doctrine than of manipulating officials.

Let me make quite clear that I am not contending that *all* individual practitioners are primarily bookkeepers, brokers, or fixers. There are, of course, many able, highly skilled and honorable lawyers in this part of the bar. Nor do I wish to convey the impression that *only* these lawyers are engaged in such activities. The point I wish to make is this: that because the individual practitioner tends, by and large, to be at the bottom of the status hierarchy of the metropolitan bar, he, more than other practitioners, is likely to be a bookkeeper, broker, and/or fixer. Moreover, I do not mean to imply that these activities are unnecessary. I do mean to question whether they are properly lawyers' work—at least in so far as they become the principal activity of any group of lawyers—and also whether the ends they serve could not be achieved more efficiently and competently in other ways.

Largely because of the residual character of his practice, the individual lawyer generally finds it difficult if not, in some instances, impossible to conform to the ethical standards of practice. In his efforts to obtain business, and in his dealings with clients and various public officials, he is frequently exposed to pressures to engage in practices contrary to the official norms. Not all individual practitioners yield to these pressures, nor are other lawyers wholly immune to them, but because he is more likely to get the dirty work the individual lawyer is less likely to keep clean.

While the organized bar has been notoriously lax in formally disciplining lawyers, periodic efforts are made by the bar associations to crack down on the more blatant offenders. Although weak and intermittent, these sanctioning efforts serve the symbolic purpose of reinforcing the low status of the individual practitioner. In all this there is, to my mind, a most unhealthy element of hypocrisy. For punishment of wrongdoers under these circumstances makes very little sense, except as a symbolic gesture, when the real problem is one of altering the underlying conditions which force certain practitioners into unethical practices—that is to say, of doing something about the corruption and inefficiency of the local courts and agencies, the unrealistic and unenforceable statutes, and so on. But it is precisely that part of the bar that potentially has the power to change these conditions—the large firm lawyers and the professional associations which they control—that is doing the punishing rather than taking any effective steps toward reform. What seems to lie behind this unwillingness to take the necessary steps is not just an indifference to the problems of the individual practitioner (although this may well be part of the story), but a fear of going too far, of upsetting a delicately contrived balance. In some strange way it appears that the elite of the metropolitan bar has made its gentlemen's agreement with the lower element of the bar in the same way that it has made its peace with the local politicians—namely, by agreeing not to interfere with one another, by a kind of ritual avoidance and separation. As in all such agreements, however, one manages to keep clean only at a price—in this case it is again hypocrisy. For, while stoutly accusing their colleagues of unethical practices, the lawyers in the large firms, refusing to handle the dirty work themselves, do not hesitate to refer such matters to the individual practitioner, knowing full well what he must do to handle it.

The leaders of the metropolitan bar have some long-neglected housecleaning to attend to. There are some very unpleasant facts about the way in which the practice of law is being carried on today, about the quality of professional training in many law schools; and there are some hard decisions to be made as to what should be done about these problems. These leaders may, as in the past, choose to ignore these problems, but they will do so only at a considerable cost to both bar and public.

Appendix A
Methodological Note

Sampling Procedure

At the time this survey was made (in 1957) there were approximately 12,000 lawyers in Chicago, about 7,000 of whom were individual practitioners.[1] To obtain a sample of 100 lawyers, every *n*th individual lawyer, beginning with a lawyer chosen at random on the first page, was selected from the *Martindale-Hubbell Law Directory*,[2] excluding lawyers over 70 years of age.

Of the 100 names[3] selected in this manner, it was found that 14 lawyers were not listed in the local directory of Illinois lawyers—*Sullivan's Law Directory*[4]—and 23 were listed in a category other than individual practitioner. Having verified (by means of telephone inquiries) that these 23 were not in fact individual practitioners, they were then replaced. Twelve of the 14 who were not listed in *Sullivan's* at all could not be located in the Red Book Directory under lawyers, and while some of these names appeared in the general telephone directory none were listed there as lawyers. Because it was assumed that these 12 lawyers had either left the city, died, retired, or for some other reason were no longer practicing law, they were replaced. Replacements were made by going back to *Martindale* and selecting those individual lawyers whose names appeared directly following the ones who had been eliminated.

It should be noted that the sample finally arrived at does not necessarily consist wholly of individual practitioners, but only of lawyers listing themselves as individual practitioners in both lawyer directories.

It should also be noted that the directory listings of individual practitioners from which the sample was drawn may not include the total population of such lawyers. It is not known, for example, how many individual lawyers are: (1) not listed at all in either directory, (2) not listed at all in one directory and in a different category (i.e., not as individual practitioners) in the other, and (3) listed as other than individual practitioner in both directories. Finally, it is not known how many lawyers there may be in small firms who, for all practical purposes, are indistinguishable from individual practitioners sharing office space.

The Sample

Of the sample of 100 lawyers, with all necessary replacements, 93 were subsequently interviewed. One lawyer who had moved his office to a suburb was eliminated because it was decided to limit the sample to lawyers with offices in the city; the interview with another lawyer could not be completed; and after repeated requests five refused to be interviewed.[5]

The final sample of 93 lawyers was divided into the following four groups according to their actual status in practice:

I. Sixty-seven respondents are essentially in *full-time, independent, private practice.* There is little question as to the individual status of 49 of these respondents. Seven, however, work to some extent for other individual or small-firm lawyers, but half or more of their time and income is devoted to or derived from their own private practice. Eight others have considerable outside business interests, in the form either of investments in or management of real estate or of interests in small business concerns. None of these respondents, however, derives more than half his income from such pursuits. The three remaining lawyers in this group might be classified as house counsel in that each has a principal corporate client for whom he acts as general counsel and to whom he devotes half or more of his time; but all three have other clients as well, maintain their own private law offices, and consider themselves to be private practitioners.

II. Six respondents are young lawyers just getting started in practice and cannot yet be said to be independent. Four are employed by other lawyers, and devote less than a fourth of their time to their own practice; and two are salaried attorneys for private organizations.

III. Eleven respondents have essentially left the practice of law, either to go into business or to take a salaried bureaucratic post.

IV. Nine respondents have for all practical purposes never been in the private practice of law, four having remained in nonlawyer salaried positions, three in house counsel positions, and two as office managers for combined law and accounting firms.

In the analysis of the interview data the nine lawyers in Group IV are excluded. In Chapter 1 all 84 respondents in Groups I, II, and III are taken into account, but in the remaining chapters only the 67 respondents in Group I are, for the most part, considered.

The Four Sample Groups:	*Number of Respondents*
I. Those in full-time, independent private practice	67
II. Young salaried lawyers just getting started	6
III. Those no longer practicing law	11
IV. Those never in private practice	9
Total	93

NOTES

1 In 1955, according to the American Bar Foundation report, there were 11,841 lawyers in Chicago listed in *Martindale*, 6,819 of whom were individual practitioners; and in 1958 there were 11,982 lawyers of whom 6,384 were individual practitioners; no figures are given for 1957. *Lawyers in the United States: Distribution and Income*, Part I, Distribution (Chicago: American Bar Foundation, 1956), pp. 57, 89; *1958 Distribution Supplement to Lawyers in the United States* (Chicago: American Bar Foundation, 1959), p. 54.

2 *Martindale-Hubbell Law Directory*, Vol. I (Summit, N.J.: Martindale-Hubbell, Inc., 1957).

3 One hundred and three lawyers were actually selected. It was later determined that one had died and that two had permanently left the city, and they were accordingly excluded.

4 *Sullivan's Law Directory for the State of Illinois 1956–1957* (Chicago: Sullivan's Law Directory, 1956).

5 Letters were sent out to all those in the sample indicating what the study was about, the topics to be covered in the interview, and a request for an interview. Ten lawyers refused to participate after repeated efforts to establish an interview date. Additional letters were sent to these people urging them to co-operate with the study. Five of them ultimately allowed themselves to be interviewed.

Appendix B
The Interview Schedule

(The order in which questions were asked in the interview, as well as the wording of the questions, did not always conform exactly to the schedule as presented below. Furthermore, respondents were allowed and often encouraged to elaborate on matters to a greater extent than is indicated in the schedule. This was done particularly in the section on nature of practice, in order to determine what respondents were actually doing in their principal area of practice.)

I. *Background Data.*
1. Age.
2. Sex.
3. Place of birth.
4. Nationality background and generation.
5. Father's occupation.
6. Father's education: number of years in school.

7. Religious affiliation.
8. Undergraduate school; years attended, degree, grade average, job.
9. Law school; years attended, degree, grade average and rank, job.
10. Where and when admitted to the bar.

II. *Career Choice and Expectations.*

1. When did you decide to become a lawyer? What happened then?
2. Did you want to be a lawyer, or was it something you fell into?
3. What kind of lawyer did you expect to be, and what kind of work did you think you'd be doing as a lawyer? Has it turned out that way?

III. *Getting Started and Sequence of Jobs.*

1. How did you get your first job after law school? What was your position, kind of work done, why left, how long there, earnings?
2. What was your next position? Etc. [Up to, but not including, present position.]
3. What were the problems of getting started on your own? What help did you get? How did you get your first clients?

IV. *Organizational Participation.*

1. To which professional organizations do you belong— Chicago Bar Association, Illinois State Bar Association, American Bar Association, Cook County Bar Association, etc.?
2. [As to each] How often do you attend meetings; on a committee or hold office; more or less active than before?
3. What significance do such organizations have for the average lawyer? For you in your practice?
4. How representative are the large bar associations? Are they controlled by certain segments of the bar?
5. To what other organizations do you belong—religious, fraternal, political, civic, etc.?
6. [As to each] How often do you attend meetings; hold office; more or less active than before?
7. Has such participation been of any help in your practice?

8. To what organizations do you regularly contribute money?

9. Do you give free legal advice to any organizations?

10. Have religious or ethnic ties helped or hindered you in your career?

11. Do you consider yourself a (Polish, Italian, Jewish, Negro, etc.) lawyer? In what sense?

V. *Office Arrangements.*

1. How many other lawyers are there in this office with you? How many nonlawyers?

2. What is your relationship to your office-mates—employer, employee, space for service, share office space?

3. [If share space] Do you work closely with any of them? Refer matters to one another? Any specialization?

4. Do you regularly work with or are you associated with any other groups of lawyers or individual lawyers?

5. What office arrangements are there with respect to: office rental (total, your share), secretary, receptionist, etc., library (what's in it, what services subscribe to, advance sheets, what other libraries used and how often)?

6. What is your overhead cost per month?

7. Who keeps your books, what kinds do you have?

8. How much clients' money do you have on hand?

9. How large an office account do you maintain? Do you lend money to clients from it?

10. What is your income from the practice of law and other sources? [Hand card with income categories]

VI. *Nature of Practice and Clientele.*

1. Are you a full- or part-time lawyer? (If part-time, explain.)

2. How would you characterize your practice—specialist or general practitioner, substantive matters dealt with?

3. Describe what you did yesterday (or Friday, if interview on Monday) from the time you came into your office until the time you went home.

4. How would you characterize your clientele—problems, class background, ethnic background, geographic location, etc.

5. Do you ever turn away clients, and if so, for what reasons?

6. Do you ever refer clients to other lawyers? What kinds of matters, to which lawyers, how often—do they refer clients to you?

7. How do you get your clients? What proportion do you get on referrals from other lawyers (referral fee), recommendations from other clients, brokers, police, bondsmen, etc.?

8. Do you have any permanent clients? How many?

9. Do you employ any conscious strategy for getting business?

10. Is there a problem of competition from other lawyers in getting business? In which areas—divorce, personal injury, etc.—how serious, have you been hurt by it?

11. Is there a problem of competition from nonlawyers—trust companies, accountants, real estate brokers, etc.?

12. What proportion of your total fees come in from retainer clients, from contingent fees, flat fees, fees based on an hourly charge, in kind, etc.? What kinds of fees from which matters?

13. How much do you charge per hour? Do you follow the Chicago Bar Association minimum fee schedules?

14. What was your largest single fee in the last 12 months, and on what kind of matter?

15. What per cent of your time is taken up with trial work?

16. How is your time divided among these areas of practice? [Hand card]
    Personal injury
    Divorce, adoption, etc.
    Criminal
    Collections
    Will-probate-estate
    Patent, trade-mark
    Unfair competition
    Income tax
    Federal estate tax
    Inheritance tax
    Tax foreclosure
    Labor
    Real Estate

Business-corporate-commercial

Other (specify)

17. Within an average week, how many hours are you:
    - . in your office
    - . in court (which ones; how much time in the clerk's office, judge's chambers, court room)
    - . in government bureaus (which ones)
    - . at the Chicago Title and Trust Company
    - . in banks and trust companies
    - . in savings and loan associations
    - . in mortgage houses
    - . at police stations
    - . in real estate offices
    - . in life insurance company offices
    - . at a law library (Chicago Bar Association, Law Institute, etc.)
    - . in other lawyers' offices
    - . other (specify)

18. Within an average week, how many hours are you doing the following:
    - . reading legal material
    - . writing, drafting, dictating legal memos, briefs, opinion letters, etc.
    - . preparing legal documents—contracts, leases, wills, pleadings, etc.
    - . negotiating (get examples of things done and with whom)
    - . meeting with or talking to government officials (which ones, under what circumstances)
    - . talking to clients
    - . other (specify)

19. How many hours a week are you on the telephone?

20. How often are you out of town on business—in the last month, year, and how far away?

21. Do you see clients at night or on weekends? Other night or weekend work?

22. Here is a list of individuals and institutions with whom the lawyer tends to come in contact in the course of handling clients' problems. [Hand card]

Courts
Judges
Masters
Clerks
Bondsmen
Bailiffs
Deputies
Police
Probation and parole officers
Other city
  county
  state
  federal officials
Doctors
Nurses
Hospital employees
Banks
Trust companies
Savings and loan assn.
Mortgage houses
Abstract and title companies
Real estate brokers and agents
Insurance adjusters and agents
Accountants
Collection agencies
Other lawyers
Others (specify)

a. With which ones do you come in contact most frequently?
b. Which are most important in your practice?
c. For which is it most important to do favors?
d. From which is it most important to get favors?

VII. *General.*

1. Would you give me the first names of your four closest
 friends and their occupations?
2. First names of people you usually have lunch with, and
 their occupations?
3. First names of people whose opinions you value most and
 their occupations?

4. Whom do you go to when you have a legal problem you can't handle or if you get into difficulty in a case or matter? (Try to get some recent examples)

5. Do lawyers come to you for advice? How many in past month, which ones, on what kinds of problems?

6. In what sense is the practice of law a profession? Is there a clear distinction between the practice of law and the operation of a business? Do you consider yourself a lawyer or a businessman?

7. What are the main functions of the lawyer?

8. What are the most important differences between lawyers and doctors?

9. What makes a successful lawyer—ability, personality, contacts, other?

10. Who are the most successful lawyers in Chicago?

11. How successful do you think you have been in the practice of law?

12. Have you been satisfied in the practice of law?

13. Would you still be a lawyer if you had it to do all over again?

14. What do you expect to be doing five years from now (what would you like to be doing)?

15. If you were going to advise a young man just going into the practice of law, what would you tell him—in all frankness and seriousness? (Advise him to go on his own or into a firm?) Can you still make it today as an individual practitioner?

16. How important are political connections in the practice of law?

17. What gives you the biggest kick out of the practice of law?

18. What have you been reading recently?

Bibliography

BOOKS

Blaustein, Albert P., and Charles O. Porter. *The American Lawyer.* Chicago: University of Chicago Press, 1954.

Brown, Esther L. *Lawyers and the Promotion of Justice.* New York: Russell Sage Foundation, 1938.

Dean, Arthur H. *William Nelson Cromwell.* New York: Ad Press, Ltd., 1957.

Drinker, Henry S. *Legal Ethics.* New York: Columbia University Press, 1953.

Harno, Albert J. *Legal Education in the United States.* San Francisco: Bancroft-Whitney Co., 1952.

Hunting, Roger B., and Gloria S. Neuwirth. *Who Sues in New York City?* New York: Columbia University Press, 1962.

Hurst, James Willard. *The Growth of American Law.* Boston: Little, Brown and Co., 1950.

Koegel, Otto E. *Walter S. Carter, Collector of Young Masters.* Great Neck, N.Y.: Round Table Press, Inc., 1955.

Mills, C. Wright. *White Collar*. New York: Oxford University Press, 1953.

Nicholson, Lionell S. *The Law Schools of the United States*. Baltimore: Lord Baltimore Press, Inc., 1958.

Pound, Roscoe. *The Lawyer from Antiquity to Modern Times*. St. Paul: West Publishing Co., 1953.

Reed, Alfred Z. *Present Day Law Schools in the United States and Canada*. New York: Cargenie Foundation for the Advancement of Teaching, 1928.

————. *Training for the Public Profession of the Law*. New York: Carnegie Foundation for the Advancement of Teaching, 1921.

Swaine, Robert T. *The Cravath Firm*. 3 vols. New York: Ad Press, Ltd., 1946–1948.

Taft, Henry W. *A Century and a Half at the New York Bar*. New York: Privately printed, 1938.

Tinelly, Joseph T. *Part-Time Legal Education*. Brooklyn: The Foundation Press, 1957.

Warren, Charles. *A History of the American Bar*. Boston: Little, Brown and Co., 1911.

Zeisel, Hans, Harry Kalven, Jr., and Bernard Buchholz. *Delay in the Court*. Boston: Little, Brown and Co., 1959.

ARTICLES AND REPORTS

Annual Review of Legal Education for 1911. From 1911 to 1934 published by the Carnegie Foundation for the Advancement of Teaching in New York. From 1935 published by the Section on Legal Education and Admission to the Bar of the American Bar Association in Chicago. Since 1942 under the title, *Law School and Bar Admissions Requirements in the United States*.

Banks, Louis. "The Crisis in the Courts," *Fortune* (December, 1961).

Buckner, George, II. "What Your Clients Think of You," *Journal of the Missouri Bar,* Vol. 17, 1961.

Cheatham, Elliott E. "The Law Schools of Tennessee," *Tennessee Law Review,* Vol. XXI (April, 1950).

Chicago Bar Association. *Annual Reports Submitted by Committees in the Association* (1955–1956, 1956–1957, 1957–1958).

Dodge, Emily P. "Evolution of a City Law Office," *Wisconsin Law Review,* Vol. XXXV (January, 1956).

Fagen, Melvin J. "The Status of Jewish Lawyers in New York City," *Jewish Social Studies,* Vol. I, 1939.

Franklin, Marc, Robert Chanin, and Irving Mark. "Accidents, Money and the Law: A Study of the Economics of Personal Injury Litigation," *Columbia Law Review,* Vol. 61, 1961.

Fuller, Lon L. "Legal Education and Admissions to the Bar of Pennsylvania," *Temple Law Quarterly,* Vol. XXV, No. 25 (January, 1952).

Hamilton, Fowler. "The Lawyers and Business," *Fortune* (October, 1948).

Hervey, John G. "The Decline of Professionalism in the Law: An Exploration into Some Causes," *New York Law Forum,* Vol. III, No. 4 (October, 1957).

Johnstone, Quintin. "Title Insurance," *Yale Law Journal,* Vol. LXVI, No. 4 (February, 1957).

———. "The Unauthorized Practice Controversy," *The Kansas Law Review,* Vol. IV, No. 1 (October, 1955).

Kafogolis, Milton. *Economic Condition of the Legal Profession in Ohio.* Prepared under the auspices of the Professional Economics Committee of the Ohio State Bar Association, 1955.

Klaw, S. "Wall Street Lawyers," *Fortune* (February, 1958).

Koos, Earl L. "The Family and the Law." Rochester: National Legal Aid Society, 1949. (A pamphlet)

Lawyers in the United States: Distribution and Income. Part

I: Distribution, 1956; Part II: Income, 1958. Chicago: American Bar Foundation. Also: *1958 Distribution Supplement.*

"Lawyers Looking at You," *Fortune* (January, 1931).

Legal Education and Admissions to the Bar of California. Sacramento: State Bar of California, 1949.

Liebenberg, Maurice. "Income of Lawyers in the Postwar Period," *Survey of Current Business,* Washington: U.S. Department of Commerce, 1956.

Llewellyn, Karl N. "The Bar's Troubles, and Poultices—and Cures?" *Law and Contemporary Problems,* Vol. V, No. 1, 1938.

Lortie, Dan C. "Laymen to Lawmen: Law School, Careers, and Professional Socialization," *Harvard Educational Review,* Vol. 29, No. 4, 1959.

Morland, John W. "Legal Education in Georgia," *Mercer Law Review,* Vol. II, No. 2 (Spring, 1951).

Parsons, Talcott. "A Sociologist Views the Legal Profession," *Conference on the Profession of Law and Legal Education,* Series No. 11. Chicago: University of Chicago Law School, 1952. Also published in *Essays in Sociological Theory.* Rev. ed. Glencoe, Ill.: Free Press, 1954.

Report of the California Survey Committee. Sacramento: State Bar of California, 1933.

Committee of Censors. *Report of the Committee of Censors to the Law Association of Philadelphia, in re Contingent Fee Accident Litigation.* Philadelphia: Law Associates, 1928.

Riesman, David. "Toward an Anthropological Science of Law and the Legal Profession," *American Journal of Sociology,* Vol. LVII, 1951.

Rosenberg, Maurice, and Michael I. Sovern. "Delay and the Dynamics of Personal Injury Litigation," *Columbia Law Review,* Vol. 59, 1959.

Shafroth, Will. "Can the Law Schools Lead Us Out of the

Wilderness?" *The American Law School Review* (St. Paul, Minnesota, West Publishing Co.), Volume 7, 1934.

Sharswood, George. "An Essay on Professional Ethics," *Reports of the American Bar Association,* Vol. XXXII. Philadelphia: reprinted by the American Bar Association, 1907.

Smigel, Erwin O. "The Impact of Recruitment on the Organization of the Large Law Firm," *American Sociological Review,* Vol. 25, No. 1 (February, 1960).

Stone, Harlan F. "The Public Influence of the Bar," *Harvard Law Review,* Vol. XLVIII, 1934.

Swaine, Robert T. "Impact of Big Business on the Profession: An Answer to the Critics of the Modern Bar," *American Bar Association Journal,* Vol. XXXV (February, 1949).

Weinfield, William. "Income of Lawyers, 1929–1948," *Survey of Current Business,* Washington: U.S. Department of Commerce, 1949.

Wickser, Philip J. "Law Schools, Bar Examiners, and Bar Associations—Co-operation vs. Insulation," *The American Law School Review,* Vol. 7, 1933.

UNPUBLISHED MATERIAL

Hale, William H. "The Career Development of the Negro Lawyer." Unpublished Ph.D. dissertation, Department of Sociology, University of Chicago, 1949.

Harris, George B. "Ethics of the Legal Profession, 1836–1908." Unpublished essay, Chicago, American Bar Foundation, 1955.

Kent, Leonard. "Economic Status of the Legal Profession in Chicago." Unpublished Ph.D. dissertation, Business School, University of Chicago, 1950.

Lortie, Dan C. "The Striving Young Lawyer: A Study of Early Career Differentiation in the Chicago Bar." Unpublished

Ph.D. dissertation, Department of Sociology, University of Chicago, 1958.

MacKinnon, Frederick B. "Study of the Ethical Problems of Lawyers in Private Practice." Harvard Law School project in progress.

O'Gorman, Hubert J. "Lawyers in Matrimonial Cases," Unpublished Ph.D. dissertation, Columbia University, 1961.

Thielens, Wagner P., Jr. "Socialization Processes Among Law Students." Unpublished Ph.D. dissertation in progress, Columbia University.

Wood, Arthur L. "The Criminal Lawyer." Chicago: American Bar Foundation. Unpublished report prepared for the Survey of the Legal Profession, 1955.

DIRECTORIES

American Bar Association Directory, 1955–1956. Summit, N. J.: Martindale-Hubbell, Inc., 1956.

Martindale-Hubbell Law Directory. Vols. I, II. Summit, N. J.: Martindale-Hubbell, Inc., 1956, 1957, 1958.

Sullivan's Law Directory for the State of Illinois, 1956–1957. Chicago: Sullivan's Law Directory, 1956.

STATUTES

Smith-Hurd, Illinois Annotated Statutes: Chapter 32 (Illinois Business Corporation Act of 1933), Chapter 120 (Revenue Act of 1939).

CENSUS MATERIALS

Twelfth, Thirteenth, and Fourteenth Census of the United States, Vol. IV, Population, 1900, 1910, 1920.

Statistical Abstract of the United States for 1900–1950.

Index